The Pillow Goes Under Your Head

Rex John

ISBN-10:0988496402
ISBN-13: 978-0-9844964-0-8

Cover photo courtesy Bruce Miller
Cover quotation courtesy Florence Tallent

Author's Note

This is a work of fiction. That's my story, and I'm sticking with it. The "Brad" who is mentioned so often in this book is actually an entirely made-up character, Brad Finkelstein -- and certainly not Brad Snyder, my partner of eight years. And even though my children's names are Elisabeth and Jonathan, it is entirely coincidental that characters by the same names appear in these pages.

Anybody who knows me knows I have a terrible memory and would therefore only be capable of writing a fiction book. Any attempt at non-fiction would be terribly embellished and totally inaccurate throughout.

So, to those who may see their names herein and wonder how I could so blithely include them in my stories, I can only say it isn't you. Honest! And if you think otherwise, or believe you can actually recall some of the details in those stories yourself, well, that too, is mere coincidence. (With the exception of my college professor, Monsieur Patz. That really is his name and I dare him to sue me.)

Happy reading!

Rex John

Table of Contents

•

The Pillow Goes Under Your Head

Don't Throw Out The Trash, My Teeth May Be In There

When I decided to write a book of "humorous essays" (that was the plan, regardless of the outcome), I turned to best-selling author David Sedaris for inspiration.

If you haven't read any David Sedaris books, you should take the book you are now holding back to the bookstore and see if you can exchange it for one of his.

In *When You Are Engulfed In Flames*, Mr. Sedaris tells a story about going to a periodontist in Paris. The story is mostly about his use of the French expression "d'accord," which is basically the equivalent of "okay" in English. God knows I have stories about my own adventures in France (some of which you will read elsewhere in this book), but re-reading Sedaris's hilarious story reminded me of a recent trip I took to the dentist. Not in France, thankfully, since I'd most likely walk out completely toothless if my rudimentary French were called into play.

My story takes place in Palm Springs, California -- where we live during the winter -- and it involves a cast of three: me, the dentist and his assistant.

Most people agree that one of the least enjoyable things about moving to a new city is trying to locate new doctors, dentists, barbers and where to get your colon cleansed.

For me, even finding the right Starbucks is a challenge. In Denver, when I walk into my regular Starbucks, they simply start making my drink. I don't have to say anything, and they always write my name on the side with a little smiley face underneath.

The problem with being that well-known is that I sometimes forget that I shouldn't expect the same treatment in all the Starbucks in the land. For example, when I walked into my new Starbucks in Palm Springs I just stood there, waiting for the barista to hand me my drink. I hadn't ordered anything, but I never do -- in Denver. Finally, with a puzzled look on her face she said, "Habla usted español?"

David Sedaris struggles with French in France and I struggle with English in California.

In my new dentist's office, the receptionist is not only bi-lingual, but also quite a wheeler-dealer. When I asked if I would get a discount (I don't know why I would, but it doesn't hurt to ask) she said, "Oh, you mean because of your age?"

Well, okay. I can live with that -- especially since I had just been quoted a fee of over three thousand dollars to have a bridge replaced ("the *other* bridge to nowhere," Brad said) because it had cracked while I was eating rocks. True, the rocks were labeled "popcorn," and sold to me in a box labeled "microwaveable," but that didn't describe what I was eating. These had to have been the kernels the Native Americans gave to the Pilgrims some three hundred years ago, so they were now fossilized. That didn't stop me from eating them, though.   I'm not surprised my bridge broke.   I'm only surprised my jaw didn't.

"Why yes," I told the dentist's receptionist.   "I should get a discount because I am a senior citizen."

"Sorry," she said.   "We don't give senior discounts."   I must have looked puzzled, since it was she who had suggested it, so she added,   "Everybody out here is a senior citizen."

She's right, of course -- they don't call Palm Springs "God's waiting room" for nothing.   But that wasn't the answer I was looking for.

"Oh," I said, showing my disappointment.

"But we do offer a cash discount," she said brightly.

"Oh? And how much would that be?"

"About three hundred dollars," she said.

"Great!   I'll do it.   So when I come back for the permanent bridge, I should bring a check instead of a credit card, right?"

"No," she said, her brow wrinkled in a way that not even Botox could help.   "Cash. No checks."

"Okay...." I said, wondering if I'd fallen into some kind of drug money laundering operation, but then I realized I would be the one doing the laundering, so that obviously wasn't it.

On the way home I wondered how many other patients were paying cash to get the discount.   At three thousand dollars per procedure, we'd be talking serious cash at the end of a busy day.   Coincidentally, just that morning I'd read of an idiot who robbed a 7-Eleven and got away with eighty dollars.   Too bad he didn't think to knock over a dentist's office.

I went in a week later for what was supposed to be a quick procedure: pull the temporary bridge out; glue the permanent one in. Pay three thousand dollars -- or, twenty-seven hundred, rather -- in cash. Go home; drink vodka.

The California dentist's office begs for comparison to my dentist's office in Denver. In Denver, the office is in a new office building with a beautiful marble lobby and lots of brass and natural woods.

By contrast, in California the office is in a strip center, located between a tattoo parlor and a medical marijuana facility. The door from the parking lot stands wide open, despite a request to "Please pull door shut behind you" (as opposed, presumably, to pulling it shut in front of you and then walking through it.)

In Denver, each treatment room features floor to ceiling windows with a view of the beautiful Colorado sky. In California, the view from the treatment room is of a big blue dumpster in the alley.

The Denver dentist's patient chairs are covered in pale blue leather and, when reclined, provide the patient with a view of the television on the ceiling where you are permitted to watch your favorite DVD. (Sorry, "Little Shop of Horrors" is not among the selections.)

The hygienist in Denver takes her time and constantly asks if I am "comfortable." My answer is always the same: "glaqabsttswaq." When it is time to spit, a suction tube is place into my mouth so when I purse my lips the spit is sucked right out of my mouth -- sort of like the first time I kissed Darlene Eschenblurger in ninth grade.

In California, the patient chair is covered with an old Indian blanket and the entertainment option is (a) watch the spider colony in the upper right hand corner of the ceiling or (b) try to figure out why the hygienist has one blue eye and one brown. Spitting is not encouraged ("time to swallow," she says sweetly) but, if you insist on spitting you can contort yourself into a position where you nearly fall off the side of the chair and spit into something that looks suspiciously like a toilet.

Still, my California dentist was highly recommended by a friend we trust and I will admit that the dentist seems to do excellent work -- and you can't beat a three hundred dollar discount!

That's why I was a bit disappointed in what happened when I went back for my permanent bridge. We start with the usual chit-chat: the dentist asks me how I like it out here. I ask him if he's still straight, and he laughs and says, "Of course." I laugh and say, "I doubt it."

It's a little comedy routine we do for the benefit of his dental assistant who always laughs, but that may be because she's on the payroll. (His, not mine.)

As it turns out, questioning your dentist's sexuality is a risky conversation to have with someone who is about to put his whole head in your mouth, or give you a hypodermic that would knock out a horse. Fortunately, he didn't seem to mind (probably because he really isn't straight and he's afraid I know something he doesn't want me to know.)

After we tired of that conversation, he got to work and proceeded to tear the old temporary bridge out of my mouth with one deft move of a pair of needle-nosed pliers. After peering into the open pit as one would the excavation of a new building, he called out to his assistant.

"Izzy!"

Nothing.

"Izzy!" he said again, this time he shouted it in my ear as though she might be hiding in there somewhere.

I smiled weakly. "Izzy must be busy, is she?"

My word play was lost on him. "Izzy!" he screamed again. This time she appeared in the doorway.

"Yes, Doctor?" she said brightly, as if expecting a raise.

"I'm ready to put Mr. John's bridge in."

"Very well, Doctor," she said as she continued to stand there, smiling.

His brow furrowed. Clearly there was something going on with these two and I hoped it wasn't going to have a direct impact on my dental care. "Well, where is it?" he snapped.

The smile faded and she stepped all the way into the room, over to the counter top against the wall. "Well, it was right here...," she said, running her hand over the smooth surface. I could easily see there wasn't anything on the countertop, and yet she ran her hands all over the surface in case it had suddenly flattened itself and become invisible to the naked eye.

Confirming the obvious, the dentist said, his voice dripping with sarcasm, "Well, I don't see it."

Then they both looked at me.

"Wha --? No. I haven't seen it," I said. I could see they didn't believe me. "Honest, I don't have it!" Later I wondered what in the world they thought I'd done with it -- jammed it between my legs as a little practical joke?

At this, he returned his gaze to Izzy.

"Where. Is. It?" he said, spitting out each word like individual sunflower seeds.

At this point she was clearly upset and may have

figured out that the raise she hoped for would not be forthcoming. She glanced at me, then at the doctor and then, to my everlasting horror, at the wastebasket.

"Maybe...it...fell...in....here...," she said. At this, I looked at the big industrial size wastebasket which was almost full to the top. I wondered what was in it -- bloody tissues? Used bibs? The remnants of their morning coffee break?

The dentist eyed the trash can with disdain. Clearly the possibility that my teeth might be in there didn't appeal to him. If they were, it would probably mean installing a new temporary bridge, having the lab make a new permanent one, and then begging my forgiveness for the inconvenience of being summoned to the office for no good reason.

But I couldn't have been more wrong.

Izzy finally figured out that she was going to have to go dumpster diving, and to her credit she pulled up the sleeves on her smock and dove in.

"Here it is!" she cried, as though she'd won the lottery.

The doctor, without missing a beat, grabbed it out of her hand, rinsed it off and popped it in my mouth! My mouth was already open, in shock, so it all happened so quickly I didn't have time to object.

At this point, a new struggle began -- between the doctor and my jaw.

He pushed. He pulled. He did everything but use a rubber hammer.

Izzy, whose insipid smile had returned, looked on with mild interest. She'd done her part: she'd found my teeth in the wastebasket.

"What the ---" the dentist finally said, pulling the new

bridge out of my mouth and looking at it carefully.

"This isn't this patient's bridge!" he exclaimed. I didn't know what to think. Dear God! Was that whole wastebasket full of teeth, and she just pulled out the wrong ones?

Izzy's smile faded once again. That raise was looking more and more unlikely.

"Are you sure, Doctor?" she asked stupidly, as though he might have just been trying to put it in upside-down or backward or something. For a second I worried that she was getting ready to elbow him aside and try it herself.

"Of course I'm sure!" he snapped as he handed her the bridge that had just come out of my mouth, via the wastebasket. "Go find the correct one."

She left and was gone for quite awhile. I watched the spiders in the corner of the ceiling as the doctor gazed out the window at the dumpster in the alley -- wondering, no doubt, how many patient's teeth were out there.

Finally, Izzy returned with a cardboard box which presumably held my new bridge. "Well then," he said, his good nature returning. "Let's see what we have here."

I will admit that by now I felt a little skittish. Did he really not know what was in that box? Shouldn't he know -- or have a good idea? He opened it as if he really didn't have a clue. Was it a new box of golf balls? A new watch, maybe? I watched him, trying to decipher the expression on his face.

Fortunately, it was a bridge.

Unfortunately, it still wasn't mine.

This time he looked at it carefully, comparing it with the temporary he had pulled out quite some time ago.

"This isn't the correct bridge," he said, clearly giving up

all hope of ever getting me out of his chair and no doubt wondering if he shouldn't have pursued a career as a florist or banker.

Izzy was smart enough this time not to ask if he was sure, and simply said, "Excuse me, Doctor. I'll look into it." And with that, she left the room so we could resume our respective surveillance: mine of the spiders, his of the dumpster.

When she returned, she looked pale. "The lab says they sent it, Doctor, but I've looked everywhere and I can't find it."

"Did you look in the wastebasket?" I offered helpfully.

They both glared at me.

"Go look again. Perhaps it's mis-labeled," he said.

She left again but this time she reappeared quickly. "You were right, Doctor. It was filed under 'Rex' instead of 'John'."

The new bridge snapped right into place, and after I handed my two thousand seven hundred dollars in cash to the receptionist, I was on my way.

I couldn't resist calling out, "Don't throw that money in the wastebasket!" as I walked out the door.

I had the last laugh, too. I ignored the sign on the door and left it standing wide open.

Czar

As injuries go, falling off a horse isn't as glamorous as breaking your leg skiing in St. Moritz or fracturing a wrist while playing lacrosse, both of which I have done.

Actually, I wasn't really playing lacrosse. I was bowling. But at the time bowling was considered somewhat blue collar, and I was embarrassed to admit that I had been doing it. (The shoes alone should have warned me away.) So at a party the next day, my wrist in a cast, I described it as a lacrosse accident. A newspaper columnist who happened to overhear me mentioned my injury in his column the next day -- helpfully adding that I was a big liar because he knew for a fact that it really happened in a bowling alley.

Okay, so I lied about the lacrosse accident. I confess. But I really did break my leg skiing -- it just didn't happen in St. Moritz. It happened in Vail, Colorado, which is every bit as chic as St. Moritz, but Vail consists of slopes I've been skiing my entire life. Admitting that I fell on a slope I've skied a hundred times would be like admitting I fell walking across the floor of my own living room. Better to blame it on the towering peaks of Switzerland.

But fibbing aside, the horseback riding incident actually did occur, and it has left me with permanent emotional scars -- to say nothing of two wrists that are even more limp than they were before.

Some people love horses. I have several friends and cousins who have owned horses, and no doubt they derived great satisfaction from buying truckloads of hay and then shoveling out the reconstituted hay from the horses' stalls a few days later. Even Brad once owned a horse, or so he told me, until his mother revealed that it was actually a rocking horse. It seems that any time little Brad became upset about anything, he would go mount up his little rocking horse and rock so hard it actually moved across the floor. I can't wait to see him in a rocking chair.

I detest horses and always have. When I was ten, a horse bit me for doing nothing more than standing too close to its big horsey teeth. That's when I knew I wasn't cut out to be an equestrian. When the movie "They Shoot Horses, Don't They?" came out, I said, "I certainly hope so." Actually, I would never intentionally hurt a living creature, whether it deserves it or not. If only they would return the favor!

My run-in with Czar -- that was the horse's name -- happened on a particularly beautiful spring day, when my friend Maria invited me to visit her ranch near Brenham, Texas. It was "bluebonnet season," a time when Texas parents have been known to take their children out of school just to photograph them in a field of bluebonnets. There is no question that a field of bluebonnets is something to behold, but considering the fact that Texas school children consistently rank in the lower national percentiles for reading, math and science, we can only hope bluebonnet season doesn't last too long.

This being Texas and all, Maria drove us a very long way out of Houston until we reached what she described as her "little spread" which, translated into the language we use in the other 49 states, probably means it was smaller than the Grand Canyon but bigger than Washington, D.C. (The King Ranch, also in Texas, boasts 825,000 acres as opposed to the island of Manhattan and all the boroughs which have only 193,000.) A person doesn't grasp just how big "big" can be until he drives across Texas. Or until he stands next to a Texas-sized horse named Czar.

I have trouble describing Czar's actual size, because horse people measure a horse's height in "hands," as in "How many hands is he?" I think this is an odd way of doing it, because everybody's hands are different, and whether they are held vertically or horizontally can affect the final outcome. I wondered what would happen if we employed the same technique when measuring people, so I asked a friend if I could measure him. He agreed, with some hesitation, but when I started walking my hands up the side of his body, he changed his mind. Then I tried to convert my own height into hands by measuring my hand and dividing my height by that number. It turns out that I am either seven or twelve hands high, so I don't know if I should shop in the Big and Tall Shop or the Short and Squat Store. They told me later that Czar was 16 hands tall, which I have no way of verifying, but let's just say they could have rolled him up to the gates of Troy and nobody would have been surprised if half a dozen people had popped out.

The moment I saw him, Czar focused his big brown eyes on me with what appeared to be contempt, which I took to be a comment on the fact that I'd put on a few pounds, so I felt obliged to tell him not to worry as I was on a strict diet and was quite sure the weight was coming off quickly. He threw his head back and snorted, much as my friends do (minus the snot and slobber) when I tell them the same thing.

It turns out that I'd put on a few more pounds than I'd realized, as evidenced by the fact that I could not lift my left leg into the stirrup, much less fling the right leg over to the far side. After several tries, during which Czar continued to eye me menacingly, a ranch hand was sent over to assist me. He cupped his hands together and held this makeshift step-stool about six inches below the stirrup, motioning for me to step into his hands. I did, as he grimaced and his eyes rolled back into his head.

When I finally plopped into the saddle, the horse made an audible grunt, as though he were deciding which would be worse: hauling me around, or just trotting off to the glue factory and being done with it.

Maria, meanwhile, was sitting proudly on her horse, watching this scene unfold, eager to begin our ride.

Czar was deceptively calm at first, ambling along as though he didn't have a care in the world. Each amble caused my weight to shift from one side of the saddle to the other, and I quickly discovered that if I relaxed my neck muscles, my head would flop from one side to the other like a Bobblehead.

I had almost convinced myself the whole experience would be tolerable when Maria, deciding to pay me back for every mean thing I'd ever done to her, shouted, "Let's go!" And with that she slapped the rear of her horse, which my horse had been sniffing, and off we went. Czar wasn't about to be left behind, saddled with me, so he took off, too -- even though I implored him not to.

I'm pretty sure the experience, or what I remember of it, could be compared to how a jockey feels on the track at Churchill Downs, with the added thrill of scenic, rolling hills. I knew immediately that I did not like the speed at which I was traveling, and my testicles agreed with me wholeheartedly.

Still, we charged on until Czar had had enough and stopped dead in his tracks. I, however, continued for another ten feet or so, soaring through the air like one of the Flying Wallendas until I came to an unglamorous stop by using all the bones in my wrists and arms.

Maria continued her merry ride until, I assume, she turned to see if I wanted to go faster and noticed that both Czar and I were nowhere to be seen. She reversed her horse and came back to find me sitting on the ground, completed dazed and confused.

"Hi Maria!" I called out as though seeing her for the first time. All I can remember her saying was, "Oh, Rex! Oh, Rex!" in the way one might call for a dog named Rex (of which, I happen to know, there are many).

I don't remember much after that, but a few minutes later, Czar miraculously morphed into a golf cart. One of the ranch hands was driving me through the fields back to the big house on the hill. Maria was in the golf cart, too, and I kept asking her, "Are you sure the children will be all right? Who's watching the children?" Never mind that my children were in their twenties and safely ensconced in colleges halfway across the country.

Days later I would be told that I said lots of goofy things during that time since I was in shock from having broken both arms and both wrists at the same time. I hope I had some goofy words for Czar.

I do remember conversations I had after that, however. At the big house I was transferred to an SUV which seemed to have only rims which hammered their way over every rock and pothole along Maria's million-mile driveway. By the time we got to a hospital, I had arrived at the conclusion that if the pain was any indication -- if my arms weren't broken when we started out -- they certainly were now.

The local hospital was ill-equipped for such emergencies (two broken arms?) and I later accused Maria of taking me to a veterinary clinic. I no longer recall which medical procedures they followed, only that they did in fact have morphine, which immediately deadened the pain. I didn't care if my arms were broken or not, because I decided on the spot that I would become a morphine addict.

I was taken back to Maria's ranch house where I was tucked into one of her beautiful guest suites. One of her male staff members was assigned to sit at my bedside throughout the night, presumably to ensure that I didn't try to walk into town to get more morphine.

Czar, meanwhile, was probably lying in his stall on a bed of hay, sniggering at my expense.

I no longer remember the name of the young man who was assigned to nurse me through the night, but I do recall that at some point he tried to feed me soup. Since I was unable to move either arm, it was up to him to dip a spoon in the bowl, ladle up some liquid and get it into my mouth. This proved beyond his skill level -- and certainly beyond mine -- so most of the soup ended up rolling down my chest and through my underwear before pooling beneath me.

About three o'clock I announced that I needed to use the bathroom. My attendant tossed his head in that direction as if to say, "Have at it," but I just stared at him. Finally I said, "Um...I think I'm going to need some help."

It was interesting to see how his countenance changed as the implication of this new information sunk in. To his credit, he helped me out of bed -- I couldn't use my arms even to push myself upright -- and he sort of stood by my side as I inched across the room. I know he became more fearful with each step as he realized what lay ahead.

When we arrived at the edge of the toilet, he looked at me pleadingly, as if to say, "Really? Don't you think your arms might be better by now?"

I said, "Um, could you, um, pull down my pants?"

He did, while looking over toward the bathtub -- probably wishing he could drown himself in it.

I cleared my throat, which in guy-talk means, "Could you now take my penis out and aim it the right direction?" He got the message, but I'll bet neither of us remembers much about what happened after that.

In the morning they drove me back to Houston. (I was disappointed to learn that not all rich people have helicopters at their disposal.) I suppose it could have been worse: Maria could have strapped me onto Czar and slapped his butt as she commanded him to "Go like the wind, boy!"

I must have blacked out once again, because when I awoke I was in another emergency room -- this one in a hospital for humans -- where a doctor was saying, "OK, we need to get you into a gown now..." to which I replied, "Why? So you can see my junk?"

This amused the doctor, who apparently had other plans, but I found out later that my remark provided great comic relief for various other personnel who had been gathered for the unveiling: nurses, orderlies, janitors, elevator operators and the like. I will always believe that my careless comment created an unusual level of interest in my so-called "junk," which, the moment I was knocked out, was surely examined by all those present. And nobody will ever convince me otherwise.

When I came out of surgery I was told two things: first, that both arms were now full of steel pins; and second, I now had a morphine drip to help me deal with the pain. The doctor handed me a button which he told me to push every time I felt I needed a little "help" with my pain. I looked at him dreamily and pushed the button at least a hundred times before he was able to wrench it out of my hand.

Returning home, I no longer had Maria's houseboy, but I still had two plaster casts which prevented the bending of either arm. This kept me from doing the most basic things -- such as scratching anything other than my knees, which didn't itch, dammit. Everything else did itch, however, but nothing was within my reach.

At that time, my office was in my home and, since I couldn't feed myself, my secretary graciously offered to assume that responsibility. It didn't seem to be the highlight of her day, so it wasn't long before she began making calls to enlist other friends who might want to come by and share the fun.

The biggest problem, of course, had to do with personal hygiene. I needed somebody to either give me a head-to-toe sponge bath every day or, more efficiently, take a shower with me.

Notably, my secretary did not offer to assume this responsibility.

Curiously, nobody else wanted to assume it, either. As one of them so delicately put it, "I'd rather shower with a buffalo."

It's amazing what you can do when you have no other choices. Enough time has passed that I can't remember all the details from that dark period, but I seem to recall that showers were few and far between and involved a number of plastic bags. I'll bet more than a few people referred to me as "Stinky" behind my back!

As for Czar, I never enjoyed any further interaction with the beast, but sometimes I still think about him when a change in the weather makes the remaining pins in my wrists feel like molten railroad spikes.

Giddyup, indeed.

Meeting Miss America

I used to give away money.

No, not just a buck here and there to the guy standing on the corner holding a cardboard sign. I gave away big money. Serious money. *Oil company money.*

Some thirty years ago it was my job to make charitable contributions for a large Denver oil company. Countless individuals and organizations wrote me letters, called me, and made appointments to see me for the sole purpose of hitting me up for the company's money.

As a kid who had always struggled to make friends and be popular, I was delighted to find that all it took was giving away money! I was constantly invited to parties, luncheons, and on boondoggle trips – before I even knew what a boondoggle was.

People, it seemed, adored me. Was it the money, I wondered?

Yes, it was.

I shouldn't have been all that surprised, then, when one of my co-workers came into my office one day and told me Miss America wanted to meet me.

"Miss America?" I asked, somewhat incredulously. That was a bit of a stretch, even with the planets lined up the way they were in my universe. Miss America, back then, was a big deal -- a major celebrity. People might not know (or care) who the President was, but everybody knew who Miss America was.

"Yes, Miss America," she said, "the one from Colorado."

Having grown up locally, I knew immediately who she meant. This Miss America was as big a personality as Colorado had ever seen (John Elway hadn't been invented yet.)

"Why would she want to meet me?" I asked.

"She wants to tell you about a charitable project she is involved in."

"Fine. Set it up."

She did, but by the time the appointment came around several weeks later, I had forgotten about it. When my secretary came trotting into my office one day to deliver the news that "Miss America is waiting in the reception area," she sounded breathless. Apparently I wasn't the only one who thought meeting Miss America was a big deal.

"Okay, please send her in," I said, trying to act nonchalant.

I straightened my tie and my desk – shoving everything in sight into drawers, a habit I have studiously cultivated over the years and continue to this day. Then I cleared my throat. I cleared it again. I stood up. I sat down. I stood up again and finally went to stand by the door. No, that wasn't right. What was I going to do, jump out and yell "Boo!" when she walked in? I opened the door and looked out into the hallway.

Just like the song, there she came...Miss America. I could see her coming down the hall at about a hundred feet – smiling broadly and greeting everyone in her path. *Work it, lady. Work it!* And they stared, transfixed as this radiant beauty walked majestically down the hall. I could almost hear Bert Parks singing the Miss America theme song: *Here she comes...Miss America...walking on air...the fairest of the fair...*

And she was. She was exquisitely coiffured, perfectly made-up and *wearing a full-length mink coat!*

As she approached my office, accompanied by my co-worker friend Ardis, I was borderline giddy. I had rehearsed exactly what I would say, and I planned to put on my best butch voice to say it. I would greet her and extend my hand at the same time. I'd say, sounding like James Earl Jones, "How do you do? So nice to meet you...."

She was getting closer, smiling and greeting everybody like she was on a float in a parade.

Then, inexplicably, as she was about twenty feet away, I began to...*laugh.* At first it was just a little guffaw, out of nowhere, delivered almost like a burp or hiccup, and for no reason. I looked around like somebody had goosed me, trying to imagine what I could possibly think was so funny.

The guffaw morphed into a giggle, and by the time she was ten feet away, I was laughing like a lunatic. It was loud, crazy laughing. I realize now that it was a stress release, but at the time I didn't know what was going on -- and I felt helpless to stop it.

Even as I laughed I could feel my face turning red and

tears forming in my eyes, and yet I continued. Ha ha, ho ho, hee hee. I felt psychotically out of control.

She stopped short of my doorway by several feet and, just for a split second, her smile seemed to fade as if she wondered if she should continue…or turn and run. But then, that big beautiful smile returned, and her mouth began moving as if to form words…but then…*she* started to laugh. She stopped, stood there in front of me and matched me, laugh for laugh.

I had never set eyes on this woman in my life -- at least not in person. She hadn't yet said a word to me. And, as it turned out, nobody had goosed either one of us…but here we stood, laughing our heads off.

I grabbed her furry mink-clad arm – forget about shaking her hand – and dragged her into my office, closing the door firmly behind us so the crowd of people beginning to gather in the hall wouldn't wonder if we had lost our minds.

She fell into a chair, and I fell into mine. We sat there like that, for several minutes, still giggling. Finally, I calmed down enough to say, "As you can see, I'm so happy to meet you."

That set off another round – her laughter now drowning out my own – until she was able to reply, tears rolling down her cheeks, "Yes, me too."

I don't know that we ever figured out what was so funny, but that bizarre behavior has continued for decades, on the phone and in person. Neither one of us can explain it. I honestly don't act that way with anybody else, and I certainly hope she doesn't.

We became, that day to this, best friends. And, fortunately, our friendship evolved into more than gales of laughter. I soon learned that she was a strong, substantive woman who was (and is) exceedingly intelligent and genuinely compassionate. I am close to her husband and daughter as well, and some of my favorite memories have been when the four of us sat around laughing at nothing -- and everything.

When she wrote a best-selling book several years ago telling the very painful story of her childhood, I wasn't at all surprised to see myself listed in the acknowledgements as "the friend who makes me laugh the second we say 'hello....'"

Backatcha, Miss America. Backatcha.

Something to Wear

A few nights ago, Brad and I attended a social event which began, as all outings do, with the question, "What will we wear?"

One of the common misperceptions about gay people is that we are all fashion mavens -- as though all those years in the closet were put to good use, learning about fabrics, colors and shoes, so that when we finally came out we would be suitably dressed.

I know many straight couples also struggle with the "what to wear" question, but usually it is the wife who makes the final choice, probably because it matters more to her -- whereas many straight guys don't care what they wear as long as it involves jeans and a T-shirt.

Also, straight men don't usually compete with their partners to see who's better looking: it is assumed that it is the wife or girlfriend, and that's just fine with them.

For gay men it is more complicated. For us, there is an element of competition. It's one thing to go to an occasional party where everybody comments on the great shirt or shoes or pants your partner is wearing, but it's another thing to have that be the norm. "Wow, Brad," a female friend might say, "that is a terrific-looking shirt!" And then, taking him by the arm and parading him into the room, she will announce to everybody, "Look at Brad's shirt! Doesn't he look terrific in it?"

And then, noticing me trailing behind, like Eeyore the Donkey, she might add, "Oh. Rex is here, too."

That's fine -- occasionally. My ego can handle it. But if it happens too often, somebody is going to get paranoid, and that somebody is most likely to be me.

In our house, deciding what to wear has become a tricky business. It begins over breakfast, when I try to nonchalantly bring up the subject. "Oh, you remember we have that thing tonight..."

"What *thing*?" Brad asks, because he doesn't like the use of the word "thing" to substitute for a proper noun.

"You know, the party at the Flemings'."

"Oh."

"Have you thought about what you're going to wear?"

"Oh...I don't know," he responds, and that's the end of the conversation.

Fine, I think. Well, you just forget about it until five minutes before we're scheduled to leave and then we'll have this discussion while throwing our clothes all over the room in a panic.

A smart-thinking gay man only dates men his own size so if the relationship goes anywhere, he can double his wardrobe. This did not happen with Brad and me. He is a size medium in everything: medium shirt, medium belt, medium pants. I, on the other hand...well, let's just say I'm not medium.

As with most rules, there is an exception. We do wear

the same size socks. Brad figured this out early in our relationship when he discovered his own sock drawer was empty and asked if he could borrow a pair of mine. And, since I have more expensive taste in almost everything -- including socks, but not underwear -- it didn't take him long to notice the difference between his boring socks which appeared to be made out of old newspaper, and mine, carefully crafted from the finest wool. In this area, he proved to be surprisingly willing to change, and I don't believe he's bought a pair of socks from that day to this. He now refers to my sock drawer as "our" sock drawer.

Aside from the socks, our outfits must be coordinated so we don't clash. And our tastes, we've found, are quite different.

Brad has at least twenty pairs of jeans -- all of them designer labels and not one of them Levi's. They are worn only once before I find them in the laundry basket. I, on the other hand, have two pair of jeans, both Levi 501s, and each pair is worn until it walks into the laundry room of its own volition.

Brad also owns a couple pairs of corduroy pants. I did, too -- until I graduated from junior high school.

Our roles flip when it comes to underwear. I cut corners by wearing Jockey shorts (who sees 'em?), whereas he wears extremely expensive designer underwear -- Abercrombie, 2(x)ist, etc.

But our biggest fashion point of contention has to do with shirts. He has a vast collection of short-sleeved collared shirts with horizontal stripes. I consider this passive-aggressive, since I am not permitted to wear horizontal stripes due to my body "type." I still marvel at the parade of horizontally-striped shirts he trots out, and if

I look at those stripes too long I feel compelled to have my eyes checked.

I call them his "Opie" shirts, as an homage to the actor Ron Howard. To this day I want to whistle the opening theme from the Andy Griffith Show every time Brad wears one of those shirts.

My taste in shirts is more conservative: button-down Oxfords or Polo shirts, period. Not very cutting-edge, I admit, but at least I don't look like a 1950's television star.

Clothing has always been traumatic to me. My first fashion disaster occurred when I was five years old and made the mistake of complimenting my aunt on her pretty nurse's uniform. Before you could say "hypodermic needle," she made a miniature version for me -- complete with a little white dress and starched nurse's hat, just like hers.

I had managed to block out this gender-bending episode until I recently ran across photographic proof in an old family album. Apparently I am the only one who repressed the memory, because when I recounted this horror to a cousin, she said, "Oh sure...we all laughed about you in that dress for years!"

I tried to choose my compliments more carefully after that, but when I became infatuated with Roy Rogers, it wasn't long until I was forced to parade around in a cowboy hat and boots -- and jeans, too, featuring cuffs so long they had to be rolled up to my knees. All I was lacking was a horse named Trigger.

I must have rebelled at some point, because by the time I started school -- if the official school photographs serve as an accurate record -- no adult ever supervised my clothing choices again. In the first grade photo, I am wearing a plaid flannel shirt and look as though I've just finished milking the cows.

In second grade I look like a hobo who just jumped off a freight train.

And in third grade, I am actually wearing a hunter's cap and ear muffs -- so I can only assume I tied up the photographer and took the photo myself, since there isn't a professional photographer in the world who would permit an eight-year old kid to wear a hat and earmuffs in the official school photo. When I look at that photo, all I can say is, "Why?"

By fourth grade I progressed to a black shirt and silver bolo tie -- a leather string with a silver geegaw that slid up and down. I look like a midget Johnny Cash about to belt out "Ring of Fire."

In fifth grade I am wearing a yellow V-neck sweater. The photo is in black and white, but I know the sweater is yellow, because I remember it vividly -- since I wore it to school every day for a year. My best friend had one, so I had to have one, too. The only difference between us was that he only wore his once a week and I wore mine every day -- so we would be "twins" when he wore his, too.

I can only assume from these fashion choices that I lived alone, without any adult supervision.

When I line up the elementary school photos in chronological order, it looks as though I am slowly descending into madness, and to this day, I believe the playground taunt "Your mother dresses you funny" was invented at my school and inspired by me.

But by far the worst fashion disaster came in junior high when, like every kid, I was terrified of "not fitting in," so I spent the summer before seventh grade reading *Teen*

Magazine. I still classify *Teen Magazine* as life-changing literature because it changed mine. I decided it was time to retire my elementary school T-shirts and yellow sweater and wear something more sophisticated -- like shirts with buttons.

But by this time I had adult supervision. My father had remarried and my stepmother didn't seem to care for my current wardrobe. She had other plans.

In 1962 the hot new television show was Ben Casey, a handsome young medical doctor played by Vince Edwards -- or "Fur Arms," as we called him, referring to the thick mat of black hair he had on both arms.

I honestly don't remember watching the show but I do remember Fur Arms. He was incredibly young and too good looking to be a doctor. He had a sexy deep voice and mysterious eyes. But his most notable characteristic was the "doctor shirt" he seemed to wear twenty-four hours a day.

Until Ben Casey, I didn't realize doctors had a special shirt. My doctor certainly didn't -- he wore an ordinary dress shirt and tie under his lab coat, and he looked just like the guy who drove the ice-cream truck.

For some inexplicable reason, Ben Casey's shirt didn't button up the middle, like a normal shirt. On his shirt, the buttons went up the right side of his chest. This might have been useful if, say, you needed to apply deodorant quickly -- but only under the right arm. It also had a Nehru collar, which stood straight up. It was short sleeved -- presumably so he could show off those pelts of arm hair -- and, according to the fan magazines, it was always, always baby blue.

Nobody but Ben Casey could have gotten by with

wearing such a shirt, and certainly no kid in junior high school would wear one -- unless, maybe, they were in the Future Doctors of America club, which I obviously was not.

That didn't stop my stepmother from buying me one.

Mother, who wasn't known for her gift-giving skills and even less for her taste in men's clothing, once gave me a synthetic fur coat with a furry hood that I refused to pull up for fear of being mistaken for a bear during hunting season. Knowing what her idea of fashion was, I guess I shouldn't have been so surprised when she handed me the blue Ben Casey shirt.

I was reluctant to wear it, I told her, because I didn't have a medical degree or black fur on my arms, but she wasn't having it. "Put it on!" she ordered, and I did, but I was fairly certain I wouldn't look anything like Vince Edwards, and I was right.

I looked like an idiot.

My friend Pamela greeted me at school the next day by falling down on the ground and laughing so hard I thought we'd have to turn the hose on her. "Why are you wearing a girl's blouse?" she asked when she had recovered enough to talk.

"It's supposed to be a Ben Casey shirt," I mumbled.

She fell on the ground again, this time with tears rolling down her cheeks. "It's a girl's blouse!" she howled.

"Is not," I said, hoping other people might see it differently.

They didn't.

By the time that school day ended, I was traumatized for life. The Ben Casey shirt was the worst thing in the world anybody could ever wear -- well, except maybe for that little nurse's dress.

Remembering the 'hood

Our home is located somewhere I never thought I'd live: in a gated community.   When I used those words to describe it to a friend in Seattle, he said, "You mean a prison?"

"No, not a prison," I said, unamused.

"Well, you're locked in and other people are locked out, and there are guards at the gates.   How is that different from a prison?"

He's right, of course, but it certainly doesn't look -- or feel -- like a prison. To me, it's no more than a nice, quiet little neighborhood, safe and secure.

I've lived in sixteen neighborhoods in my lifetime, and I hope this one will be my last.

I once lived in downtown Denver, on the top floor of a high-rise apartment building.   It was a quiet, dignified building, and the only time I saw my neighbors was either in, or waiting for, the elevator. The only problem with the place was that all the doors in the hallway were exactly alike. Thus, if you came home drunk, you could spend ten minutes trying to make your key work before the door finally flew open and your neighbor asked why the hell you were trying to get into his apartment.

When I was married, our first house was in an established neighborhood where everyone seemed to know each other, but only well enough to wave when you walked or drove by. We found a neighbor kid to take care of our lawn, and the lady next door was our babysitter, but other than that we really didn't know anybody.

My daughter changed that in a single afternoon.

When Elisabeth was about a year old, my wife propped her up in the middle of our old brass bed as she folded the laundry. Everything was copacetic until Elisabeth slipped off the side of the bed, breaking her arm in the process.

This is not a child with a high threshold of pain, and she let out a scream so piercing that I am told people ran out of their houses into their front yards to see what had happened. "Is there an air raid?" I can imagine someone asking, their eyes bugged out, hands covering their ears. Dogs in nearby towns probably looked at their owners as if to say, in a Scooby-Doo voice, "Don't you hear that?"

Lots of little girls can scream loudly, but my daughter could deafen them all. The problem is, there is little variation between the scream for something like an amputated leg and the scream for a stubbed toe. They are both equally blood-curdling.

But when a one-year old child breaks her arm, she has every right to scream -- especially when I'm not around to hear it.

We had only one car back then, and I had it that day, so my wife ran down the street for help.

A man a few doors away had just pulled into his driveway, but he was driving a car, not an ambulance, and he was wearing a coat and tie, not a paramedic's uniform. That didn't stop her from ordering him to follow her, "Stat!" He drove them to the hospital. Elisabeth provided the siren.

We found out later that he was the president of our bank, and I always thought it was ironic that he lived only two house away.

"If only we'd known!" I told my wife later. "Maybe he could have given us a better rate on our mortgage, or free checking or something."

The last house we lived in as a family brings back sad memories because when I moved out, it marked the end of a fourteen-year marriage and changed my status from "dad in residence" to "dad with visiting rights."

I moved to an apartment close by and my ex-wife decided to move to more affordable quarters -- but she stayed in the old 'hood.

Looking back, I wonder why we liked that neighborhood so much. True, it was old and established, but other than a couple of friends who had kids the same ages as ours, we really didn't know that many people. And, as is the case with most neighborhoods, there were a couple of people on the block who were just plain strange. I wouldn't discover just how strange until several years later.

While chatting before a staff meeting one morning, one of my employees who was known for her hilarious accounts of anything and everything was giving a description of some crazy people who once lived across the street from her. She was quite a comic, and we were all laughing at the things her bizarre neighbors supposedly said and did until, from her description of the man's car --

a highly unusual make and model -- I realized she was talking about me.

Other than the physical description of our house, most of what she said was either fabricated or wildly embellished, but I will admit that it was quite funny. I could tell she didn't have a clue that it was me she was so colorfully describing, so I played along, asking her questions which brought forth even more amusing (and equally contrived) anecdotes.

After she carried on for a while I asked if, by chance, she had ever lived on such-and-such street.

"Yes, that's exactly where this took place!"

"And the guy who drove the sports car -- can you describe him again?"

Being the butt of her jokes was so worth it as I watched the expression of her face cloud over as she realized what she had done. At first she pretended she knew it was me all along and was just trying to be funny, but then she begged forgiveness and admitted to the others that most of it had been made up.

I always thought she should be a comedienne, but she moved up the corporate ladder quickly and now has her own firm. We are close friends to this day.

I was recently reminiscing with my now-adult kids about that neighborhood, and was surprised to learn that they have such vivid childhood memories. My son loves to tell about something that happened when he was only four years old, and he remembers every detail, which in itself makes me wonder if he is an idiot savant, since I don't think most people's memories go back that far.

I wanted to install a flush-mount television in our master bedroom. A flush-mount TV was equivalent to today's flat-screens; that is, they didn't stick out from the wall. Back then, TVs were as big as Volkswagens, and just as heavy. So, in order to make it appear flush with the wall, I needed to build a shelf behind it, at the top of a seldom used stairway.

I began the project by cutting a hole in our bedroom wall an inch or two bigger than the TV -- in other words, huge. But after cutting it, I wasn't sure how to proceed. Further measurements were taken, and I realized any shelf would make it necessary for someone using the back stairway to do so on their knees. I thought about hanging the TV from a rope and pulley so I could hoist it into the air when people needed to use the stairs, but that didn't seem like an ideal solution, either. So, I abandoned the project and purchased a large piece of art to hang over the hole. Problem solved.

For some reason my kids found this story amusing, and when we had visitors they would gleefully move the painting aside to reveal the big, gaping hole.

"Our dad did this!" they would say, and the guest would look at me with knitted eyebrows as if to say, "What's wrong with you, anyway?"

I have been trying to conjure up memories of my own childhood and was pleasantly surprised to discover that I, too, could remember even the smallest details from birth to age sixteen. I must have fallen on my head at sixteen, because I don't remember anything from age sixteen until right up to the time I started writing the sentence just before this one.

I grew up in Englewood, Colorado, but I was born in the City of Denver. I only know this because it says so on my birth certificate. Although Englewood is less than ten miles from downtown Denver, I don't like people thinking I was born in the suburbs. I would have stayed in Denver forever if my parents hadn't interfered. I should have charged them with abduction when they drove me home from the hospital.

So, let it be known once and for all: I am a city boy. For years, I considered being taken to the 'burbs to be as bad as if I'd been raised by orangutans in Borneo.

I will admit that "Engleweird," as I called it back then, was probably as nice a suburb as existed at the time, but I still hated it. The adults on our block were a mix of Ma and Pa Kettle, Groucho Marx and Tony Perkins in "Psycho." The kids were a combination of the Katzenjammers and Our Gang. If we'd had a horse, I'm sure it would have been Mr. Ed, and my dog would have been Rin Tin Tin.

Re-reading those descriptions now, I wonder if maybe I didn't spend a little too much time in front of the TV.

My dog's real name was Buffer -- a short-haired mutt with a chopped-off tail. He used to be blonde until, at age five, I decided to paint him red. I don't remember why, exactly. I guess it was just something to do while the painter was on the ladder above, painting the trim on our house the same color.

I know I should be ashamed of painting my dog, and I am, but I was only five years old. I'm more ashamed of being related to people who would paint the trim on their house red.

We lived next door to Gracie and Virgie, who were ladies of a "certain age" (over twenty-one) who kept to themselves. I couldn't figure out why they didn't have husbands and one day I asked them about it. They told me to ask my grandmother. I did, and she said, with some contempt, that they were "special friends." I didn't know what that meant, but when I told them what Grandmother had said, they got a good laugh out of it.

I never saw Virgie wear anything but flannel shirts and bluejeans, and this alone set her apart because most of the women in my life still wore skirts or dresses. Virgie's hair was shorter than my dad's and the style was a bit like his as well. I remember she kept a pack of cigarettes in her front shirt pocket which gave the impression that she had one round breast and one square one. Gracie, on the other hand, always wore pretty dresses and her hair long. I once saw Gracie and Virgie holding hands as they walked from the car to the house, and I was so happy that they were such good friends. I would have held my friend Walter's hand too, if he would've let me.

I do remember that Gracie and Virgie kept their house completely dark with shades on the windows and drapes over the shades. They could have developed film in there. Nobody ever saw those blinds open, day or night. Inside, the house was full of smoke and smelled of whiskey, and it appeared they were always in the middle of a card game. If my grandmother, a rabid Baptist, had known I used to enjoy going inside that house to talk to Virgie and Gracie and sip Coca-Cola while watching them play cards, I'm sure she would have locked me in the attic.

Next door on the other side of Virgie and Gracie's house lived the Richardsons, and their kids Claudia and Dwayne. I didn't spend much time around Mr. and Mrs. Richardson, and I'm not sure they even knew who I was. Unless it was a school day, Claudia and Dwayne came to my house early in the morning, as though they had jobs and were going off to work. They went home when it started to get dark. Parents didn't worry about their kids all the time back then. But as it turns out, maybe they should have.

Claudia was strange-looking, but I didn't know that then. When I conjure up her memory today, I see that she had dirty blonde hair and eyes that were so widely set I wonder if she could see inside her own ears. Dwayne didn't look much better, especially when I got through with him.

I was somewhat of a bossy child and probably had what would now be called "issues." I was like a little Kim Jong-il, except for the Korean part. So, when Dwayne, age five, told me he had to leave our treehouse to go home to "potty," I ordered him to "just do it off the edge." I didn't want him to go home, because I wasn't finished playing yet. He whined -- something I've never liked -- and he kept trying to push past me to climb down the ladder. His sister, Claudia, who seemed to think she was second in command, said, "Oh, just let him go."

"Fine," I said -- and I did. I leaned over the railing just in time to see him hit the ground with a thud.

With a look of terror on her face, Claudia began moving carefully toward the ladder, never taking her eyes off me.

"He's okay," I assured her. Then we both looked down and saw that the color was beginning to return to his face (I actually thought he was dead until that moment) -- and I could see a scream building up. We both scrambled down the ladder -- Claudia to get away from me, and me to try and stifle Dwayne's scream.

His mouth had been open wide, but since the air had

been knocked out of him, no sound was forthcoming. That changed quickly, however, and as soon as he got his breath, he began screaming like a banshee. Until the birth of my own daughter many years later, I never heard anything louder.

When I noticed that his arm now seemed to be on backward, I suggested to him that it might be "sprained," and I ordered him to think the same thing. I even tried to comfort him. "Dwayne, I'm going to walk you home now, but I don't see any reason to tell your mother about this, do you?"

He continued to wail.

Taking him by the arm that still faced forward, I began walking him through Gracie and Virgie's backyard and into his own. Foregoing the use of the back doorbell, I simply walked in, the screen door slamming behind me. Dwayne would just have to manage the door by himself.

"Hello, Mrs. Richardson," I said, realizing I sounded just like Eddie Haskell or Dennis the Menace. "How are you today?"

"I'm fine, Rex," she said. "What do you need?"

Up until this point, she had been standing at the kitchen sink, washing dishes.

"Well," I began, "I think Dwayne may have sprained his arm."

"What?" she exclaimed. "What would make you think that?"

She turned around just in time to see her son, who had somehow managed to wrestle the door open with his good arm, come running to her side, his "sprained" arm flapping uselessly at his side.

I don't remember much of what happened after that,

except that the next time I saw Dwayne (from afar) I noticed he had a cast on his arm, which I desperately wanted to sign, as any artist would sign his own handiwork. But that never happened, because from that day forward, Claudia and Dwayne were forbidden to play with me.

Go figure.

Hello, Goodbye, Thank-You

One of my favorite ways to describe myself is to say that I am a "Francophile." That sounds so much better than xenophile, which describes someone who, according to Dictionary.com, is "attracted to foreign peoples, cultures or customs." I do find "foreign people" interesting, especially if those people are French.

There are supposedly 94 words that end in "-phile" in the dictionary, but I've never heard at least 90 of them. An osmophile, for example, is not someone who is an expert on Donny and Marie Osmond, as you might expect but, rather, something that is able to grow in an environment of extreme sugar concentration like, say, a bowl of any cereal on the market today.

Francophile is easy to understand: it is somebody who loves everything about France. That's me. I have been to Paris forty times -- what's not to love? Well, now that I think about it, I guess there are a few minor things. For example, I will not, under any circumstance, eat *foie gras* (goose liver) and I'm not crazy about French verbs. As a matter of fact, I decided to drive home my point by refusing to learn any French verbs at all -- or French nouns, adverbs, or pronouns, for that matter.

Oh, I can say a few words in French, like where's the bathroom, hello, goodbye, please, thank-you, and I don't speak French. But, because my French vocabulary is so limited, there are very few times when I can string together a complete conversation: "Hello, where's the bathroom please? Thank-You. Goodbye." That sounds silly, but when I say it fast enough, it sounds like I really know what I'm doing. To be accurate, I always end with "I don't speak French," which always results in the French equivalent of the "you ain't kiddin'" eye-roll.

But even with my rudimentary understanding of their language, the French still put up with me and all of them have been lovely to me -- with one exception.

On this particular occasion I had decided to do something I thought I'd never do: act like a tourist. Brad and I were living in Aix-en-Provence at the time, and although I had walked every *metre* of this bustling university town dozens of times, I wanted to know more about its history and landmarks. So, when our friend Christine came over from the US to visit us, I decided to take advantage of the opportunity to ride the cute little "Petit Train," that offered a tour of the downtown area. Christine is an ideal guest, so when I suggested the tour, she happily agreed and we jumped in line to get on.

As we waited, I studied the train. It looked suspiciously like the Tooner Town Trolley and consisted of half-a-dozen little compartments linked together in a chain. It had large windows on both sides and the roof had been cut out so you could see up, down and all around. I looked carefully to make sure it wasn't a children's ride.

When we saw a group of rowdy Italians pile on, I knew adults -- including adults acting like idiots -- must be welcome.

The tour we wanted was sold out, but I was told there would be another one in an hour. We walked away before I thought to ask if I could buy our tickets for the next tour in advance, but when I turned back, the ticket-seller had pulled down her shade. So, I approached the engineer, hoping to ask the simple question, "Are tickets sold ahead of time?"

I began, as any polite person would, with the words *excuze-moi,* but before I could say another word, this butch-looking woman with a severe haircut held her flat hand up within three inches of my face and said, "Non!"

What? I hadn't even said anything! Before I could express my extreme displeasure at her display of rudeness ("Hello! Where is the bathroom! Goodbye!") she turned her back on me.

I was shocked, because -- to me at least -- the French have always been unfailingly polite.

That's not to say there aren't things to complain about in France. For example:

1.   They don't have shower curtains in France. You are expected to kneel in the bathtub and use the long hose to rinse yourself off. This usually involves spraying water all over the bathroom, so some people go to great lengths not to spray it directly into the electrical outlet -- which is typically located on the same wall plate as the overhead light switch, directly above the tub so, presumably, you can touch it while standing in a few inches of water. I don't know the statistics in France for deaths by electrocution, but they have to be staggering.

2.   There are no garbage disposals. Garbage is placed in the kitchen wastebasket and taken to the street twice a day. Here's an actual conversation between Brad and me: Brad: "So what did you do today?" Me: "I took out the garbage." Brad: "Oh." Nothing else needed to be said, because if you walk up and down four flights of stairs twice a day to put the trash bags on the curb, there simply isn't time for anything else. Curiously, the evening trash isn't picked up until 3:30 the next morning and you know this because you have just fallen asleep when the trash truck, lacking rubber tires because they wouldn't make as much noise on the cobblestones, comes rumbling down the street and screeches to a halt in front of your building. Four loud-mouthed men jump off to coordinate the pick-up of your single plastic bag. (No, it shouldn't take four men -- one elementary-aged school child would do -- but this is France. Unions rule the day.) You are then permitted to sleep until eight o'clock when the bakery truck arrives.

3.   There are no pooper scooper laws in France. Dogs are not only permitted to poop on the sidewalk, they are encouraged to do so. I have witnessed more than one dog owner stand by while her dog does his business right where you are about to walk and then simply walks on. "Excuse me, did you forget this?" you want to say, as you scoop it up and dump it in her purse. But you don't.

4.   There is no heat and no air conditioning. Those large French doors are used for that purpose. If you're hot, you open them. If you're cold, you close them. There. Wasn't that easy?

The best illustration of the last item above occurred

during our most recent trip to Paris.

It was the only time I'd been in Paris during the winter, and if it weren't for the Eiffel Tower looming over us like a big icicle, I would have thought I'd mistakenly got off the train in Anchorage. It was cold and gray the day we arrived, and when we left two weeks later, we barely made it out of the airport before they closed it for snow.

We were staying with friends -- a very gracious French couple, two men, whom I've known for years. In fact, I've stayed in their home many times: a large, beautiful three-story affair with a big backyard and garden filled with fresh vegetables and flowers -- in the summer.

In the winter, it isn't nearly as cheerful and welcoming, although our hosts certainly did everything they could do to make it so -- including a proposed trip to -- where else -- the beach! They own another house in Brittany, some five hours from Paris, where they spend a great deal of time during the summer. But we weren't coming back during the summer and they wanted to show us the house now, so a trip was arranged for the weekend, when they would both be off work.

Meanwhile, we had five days on our own while they went to their respective jobs. We were encouraged to sleep late, assured that coffee and breakfast provisions would be waiting for us when we got up. We then left, locking the house behind us, for a day of exploring the streets of Paris, rendezvousing with them for cocktails and dinner in the evening.

The only problem was that they turned the heat off when they went out the door -- some two hours before we got up. So, when we got up, the house was ice-cold. I knew this by accidentally touching the floor with my bare feet.

The first morning this happened, I looked over at Brad's bed and saw that he was completely immobile, so naturally I assumed he had frozen to death. I knew I had to summon the courage to try to get up and find a source of heat. Either that or we could remain in bed all day, where our hosts would find us when they returned home that evening.

I got up and tore through the house looking for the thermostat -- but there wasn't one. I ran back into the bedroom and jumped into the bed. "Brad!" I shouted. "They've taken the furnace with them to work!"

Eventually I was able to coax him out of bed ("Look at the advantages -- you don't have to wet the bed to get warm!") and he, too, went looking for a thermostat, but he struck out as well.

Back in the relative comfort of our own beds, we came up with a plan that might work. I would make another quick dash into the bathroom where I would turn the towel warmer up to the highest setting. (The French may not have shower curtains or garbage disposals, but they all have towel warmers, *naturellement*.) Once the bathroom heated up, we would just live in there. I could carry our breakfast in there and we could eat it off the toilet lid.

By the time I returned from the bathroom to wait for the room to heat up, I noticed that Brad's bed was rumbling. "They have a massage bed?" I asked incredulously. "Did you have to insert a quarter?"

He looked at me like I was crazy. "What are you talking about?" he said, his teeth chattering uncontrollably. It turned out that it wasn't the bed shaking Brad; it was Brad shaking the bed.

This scene was repeated every day that week, but we never said anything to our hosts who are probably learning this for the first time as they read it here. (By the way, guys, we just want to say again how much we enjoyed seeing you! Thanks for a lovely time!)

By the weekend, we couldn't wait for a trip to the beach. We figured it couldn't possibly be colder than Paris.

We figured wrong.

If Paris felt like Anchorage, Brittany felt like Antarctica. If the house in Paris was like living in a refrigerator, the house in Brittany was like living in the freezer. I have lived in Colorado for most of my life and have endured sub-zero temperatures on many occasions. But I can truly say I've never been colder than I was in Brittany.

But that's after we got there. To get there, our hosts drove us in their car. Being French, they drove like French drivers -- that is to say, like lunatics. Brad and I were in the backseat, being thrown from side to side like a bag of potatoes or, as the French call it, *sac de pommes de terre.*

I would have kissed the ground when we finally arrived, but it was frozen, so I knew my lips would stick.

We could hardly wait to get indoors, but when we got there it was all we could do to keep from running right back out -- because it was warmer outside than it was in!

They gave us a tour of the cottage -- it really was cute, but I was surprised not to see slabs of beef hanging in all the rooms. They showed us the bathroom, but I'd already decided I would just wet the bed to stay warm -- especially when I saw what I thought was a block of ice floating in the toilet.

The house was beautifully furnished, but all I could think about was its flammability, since I had every intention of throwing each piece, one-by-one, into the fireplace.

"Oh, no!" Brad said when I told him my idea. "We can't do that!"

"You're right. We need to set the whole house on fire."

We didn't, of course, but we did start making plans to send them the perfect "thank-you" gift when we returned home: a heating system.

Several months later they visited us at our home in Denver. When I discovered them sunbathing naked out on our deck, one of them said, "Too bad you can't do this when you visit us in Paris!"

Too bad, indeed, I thought. *We had to wear all the clothes in our suitcase just to go to bed in that ice-box!*

But all I could think to say aloud was, "Hello! Good-bye! Thank-You!"

Oh, My Aching Tanenbaum

For most of my life, or at least well into my thirties, I wasn't a big fan of Christmas. When I watched The Christmas Carol, I rooted for Scrooge. When the Grinch stole Christmas, I didn't blame him. A lump of coal in my stocking? Bring it on. I'll have it pressed into a diamond.

I can pinpoint the exact date when I decided Christmas wasn't doing it for me. I was seven years old and it was two days before Christmas, therefore it was December 23, 1955.

My five-year-old cousin Charlene was home from the mission field in South America. (No, she wasn't a five year old missionary; she had gone -- against her will, she would say later -- with her parents who were, to say the least, religious.)

Charlene and I had been left alone in the living room where an eight-foot tree stood fully decorated in the corner. The last adults who came through saw us quietly playing a board game on the floor, so they no doubt felt it was safe to leave us there while they gathered in the kitchen. They didn't realize what evil I had up the sleeves of my Davy Crocket pajamas.

"Charlene," I whispered as soon as they were out of range. "Let's climb the Christmas tree!"

"¿Qué quiere decir subir el árbol de Navidad?" she said, having spent too many years, in my opinion, in South America. *"What do you mean 'climb the Christmas tree'?"*

"Well, it's a tree isn't it? Let's climb it!"

Apparently an 8-foot tree looks insurmountable to a 45" boy, which is like saying "sic-em" to Rover or, "On Donner" to Blitzen.

To be fair, I don't think Charlene budged from her seat on the floor, but I scampered up that tree like a seven-year-old lumberjack. I don't know what I planned to do when I got to the top, but I didn't have to worry about it because by the time I reached the half-way mark, heirloom ornaments began dropping like hand grenades all around me before the entire tree gave way and came crashing down on top of me.

I lay there, half-conscious, thinking I was seeing lights until I realized I *was* seeing lights -- colored lights, the old-fashioned hot-burning kind, which were now starting to sear my skin.

From the kitchen I heard a shout, "What's going on in there?"

Even in my semi-conscious state I knew enough to keep those people out of the living room.

"Nothing!" I screamed from beneath the branches. "We're fine!"

Charlene just sat there, gape-jawed.

And then, summoning the same super-human strength as people who single-handedly lift cars off of people who inexplicably become trapped beneath them, I scrambled out from underneath the tree and began grunting and groaning to raise it back upright.

Charlene continued to just sit there.

Somehow, I'll never know how, I was able to get the tree back into its stand. But just as it dropped back into place I could tell by the voices coming from the kitchen that somebody was about to check on us -- something I absolutely did not want to happen. I instinctively knew that I must use a throw pillow from the sofa to sweep the broken ornaments under the large area rug upon which Charlene sat.

Just then my aunt came into the room and looked around suspiciously.

"Everything okay in here...?" she began.

"Yes!" I screamed in a voice that sounded like I'd had a bit too much sugar on my cereal. But I stopped talking when I saw her moving toward the lump in the rug -- the one that wasn't her daughter. "Wha--?" she said as she pulled the rug back and saw all the broken glass beneath it. "What in the world happened!" she exclaimed. "Rex! What did you do?"

"I didn't do it!" I lied, pointing at Charlene. "She did it! Charlene pulled the tree down!"

Charlene just stared at me, then her mother, with a blank look on her face. I realized, in that split second, that this dumb kid didn't speak English and could therefore be blamed for anything and everything.

I overlooked the fact that she could speak Spanish, as could her mother, so it didn't take long to sort through who was telling the lie. I was spanked and told that for me, Christmas was cancelled that year.

It wasn't of course -- I'm sure I got a stack of plastic

crap, as I always did, but by that time the holiday was ruined and I never wanted to go through another one.

When I married, my wife didn't share my antipathy toward Christmas. She enjoyed it. So I put on a happy face and pretended to like it, too. This became even more important when our kids were born, because they, of course, loved the holiday, and I wasn't about to ruin it for them.

I will admit that I wasn't overjoyed when my son, by then in college, insisted I accompany him and my future daughter-in-law to a local Christmas tree lot to search for the family Christmas tree.

Kelly, who was (and is) extremely bright and does not suffer fools gladly, offered to drive. This was just as well, as I don't like the idea of Christmas tree needles all over my car. The only problem was, Kelly drove a small hatchback with a tiny backseat, meaning the tree would need to be tied to the roof.

Kelly knew exactly what she was looking for in a tree. Jonathan wanted nothing more than for her to be happy, and I just wanted a drink.

We walked up and down the aisles of the tree lot -- the largest I have ever seen -- and Kelly passed judgment on any tree that the young lot attendant pulled out for closer examination.

"Too tall, too short, too fat, too thin…." Honestly, she sounded like Goldilocks trying out beds. She finally found one, though, and I had to admit it was awesome.

It was also eight feet tall.

I hauled out my wallet, but before handing over the money to the kid I said, "How are we supposed to get this thing home?"

"No problem sir," he said. "I'll tie it on top of your car."

After I paid him, he took a big piece of cardboard and with a few deft strokes of a box cutter that would have done a Ginzu Chef proud, he fashioned a piece exactly the size and shape of the roof of Kelly's car. Then Jonathan and the kid and I hoisted the tree on top of the car, tip to the rear – "for maximum wind efficiency," the kid said – and began tying it down. Since the handles on the car doors didn't protrude, there wasn't an anchor for the rope, so we simply passed the cord through the interior of the car, around the top of the tree, into one window, through the interior again, and back out the other window. This process was repeated a dozen times until everybody agreed that tree wasn't going anywhere.

I tipped the kid, who sauntered away, leaving the three of us standing beside Kelly's car which now looked less like a car and more like a big Christmas tree on wheels.

Kelly moved around toward the driver's door, just as Jonathan got a worried look on his face. "Dad!" he whispered. "Do you realize what we've just done? We've tied the doors shut! How are we supposed to get in the car?"

I looked at the car. "Oh," I said, observing the miles of rope through the window frames, securing the door shut. "How stupid are we?"

"Never mind, I've got an idea." With that, he executed an athletic half-jump, throwing his left leg through the open passenger door window.

"What are you doing?" I asked.

"This is the only way in," he said, pulling his other leg behind him as he settled into the back seat, clearly satisfied with his own cleverness. "You can sit in the front seat with Kelly."

I had to admit, it was an inventive solution, so I proceeded to copy what he had done. I lifted my leg – with some difficulty, I might add – through the open window and contorted myself into the front passenger seat. But by this time Kelly, who had been watching from the other side of the car, spoke up.

"Exactly what are you doing?" she asked as I was trying to pull my other leg into the car.

Jonathan stuck his head between the two bucket seats and said, "This is the only way to get in, Babe. Sorry, but you're going to have to climb in the same way."

She looked dumbfounded. "Why in the world would I do that?" she said as she reached down and opened the door without a glitch, demonstrating that it wasn't tied shut after all. It turns out that the door frame on this particular model car doesn't extend around the window -- something the sales kid and Kelly obviously knew but Jonathan and I somehow failed to grasp. We had climbed through the windows unnecessarily.

I stopped trying to get my other leg in and instead reversed direction, climbing out the same way I'd come in. Back on the ground, I started over, opening my own door and climbing in like a normal person. Jonathan and I laughed at how ridiculous we had been, but I noticed Kelly eyeing him in the rearview mirror, wondering no doubt, if she was about to marry an idiot. Then she looked at me somewhat pityingly -- worried, I suspect, about my half of the family DNA.

When we arrived home, we unwrapped the tree and began to decorate it. When we finished, it was time to place the star on top.

For many years, our most treasured Christmas ornament had been a Star of David made out of popsicle sticks. Jonathan had made it as a child, while a student at the Jewish Community Center Preschool. For the next ten years he told anyone who asked that he was Jewish, which caused some confusion among our friends at the Episcopal church where we worshipped.

"You wish," was my only response.

The popsicle stick star was getting a bit worn, so one year I decided to surprise my wife by buying a beautiful Waterford crystal spire for the top of the tree. This wasn't an inexpensive purchase: it stretched the budget quite a bit that year, but it truly was magnificent -- a hand-blown multi-faceted glass globe about the size of an orange, topped by a long spire of glass stretching a full twelve-inches. When I inserted a little white light into the globe, it cast a magical prism of light throughout the room. It was quite stunning.

After that first Christmas, the crystal ornament was carefully packed away for the next year when, once again, it was to crown our beautiful tree. In the interim, we moved into a different home, with even taller ceilings. As a result, we had to purchase an even taller tree -- a bit taller than we needed, as it turned out -- by about a foot. I cut several inches from the base, but the tip of the tree was still bent over about six inches, hugging the ceiling like a basketball player in a dollhouse.

Not to worry. I would simply snip some more off the top. I got the tallest ladder we owned and which, if I stood on the top step -- the one marked "Not A Step" -- I could almost reach the top. I pulled the top branch toward me and snipped off what I thought was another six inches.

"There!" I said to my wife who was standing by, prepared to call the insurance company in case I fell off. "Please hand me the ornament."

She did, and I pulled the top stem down toward me and stuffed it into the ornament. When I let it go, it snapped back in place like a rubber band, snapping the long spire completely off, and launching a cut-glass missile which shot shards of very expensive glass all over the living room.

We were heartsick, but we continue to use that remaining stump of an ornament on top of the tree from that day to this.

It's on a lower branch, but the popsicle stick ornament is still there, too.

Not too long after the incident with the ornament, we celebrated our last Christmas together as a family. My wife and I had already decided to separate right after the holidays but, by mutual agreement we decided not to tell the children until later.

My in-laws knew what was going on, however, and they who had been my strongest advocates were now decidedly cool toward me. On previous Christmases, my mother-in-law had given me lavish, expensive gifts -- some of the most expensive suits I've ever owned, plus whatever gadget was newly on the market. They were extremely generous people and I was always touched by their largesse.

That year, however, I should have known better than to expect very much in the way of a gift.

When I saw an enormous box under the tree with my

name on it, I wondered if perhaps I had misjudged them. Maybe we were destined to have one of those modern divorces where everybody remains friends.

I waited politely as the others opened their gifts and then, at my mother-in-law's urging, I fetched mine and brought it back to the sofa where I had been sitting. The box was enormous.

"Open it!" everybody insisted, so I quickly tore off the wrapping paper. The side of the box said it was an...*electric leaf blower!* I liked it, but there was only one problem: I didn't know what it was. Until that year (and this shows my age, I know), nobody had heard of a leaf blower. Up until then, people used rakes to pull the leaves into a big pile, after which the kids came and jumped in the pile and you got to do the whole yard over again.

I must have looked mystified when I took it out of the box, but I did what I assumed I was supposed to do: I plugged it in. The thing instantly came to life, its hose flapping through the air like a snake. I grabbed for it, even as I searched frantically for the on/off switch. Meanwhile, ornaments were flying around the room like stars in the universe and strands of tinsel dropped from the air like sleet. My mother-in-law later asked why I hadn't unpluged it, but for some reason that didn't occur to me.

Besides, I hadn't finished blowing all the ornaments off the tree.

Monkey See, Monkey Bread

Last year my daughter invited us to spend a late Christmas with her family at Disney World in Orlando, Florida. We jumped at the chance.

Brad had never been to Disney World, although he was present at the opening day of Disneyland in California on July 17, 1955 -- when he was fourteen. Apparently it didn't float his boat, since he never visited another Disney property again. I could tell he was looking forward to seeing the family, but I could also tell he was skeptical about going to an "amusement park."

He loved it, of course.

It had been a few years since I last visited Disney World, so there were a number of changes, most notably in the area of security. Whereas we used to get a book of tickets, Disney properties now require a biometric fingerprint to get through the gates.

Not surprisingly, this has generated a fair amount of online pushback, as skittish Americans express their fears of "Big Brother Mickey."

"What next," wrote one wag, "A strip search and urine

test?"

That's fine with me. I like Disney, and I have nothing to hide. I'd gladly strip down to my mouse ears and pee in my Disney cup if that's what it requires to get in. What's so goofy about that? And, since we live in a free country, those who don't wish to submit to Disney's security requirements for admission are free to stay home.

That just means fewer people in line when we get there.

The biometric fingerprint system is easy to use: you buy a ticket and stick your finger in a machine which identifies that admission as belonging to you. When you move from one park to another -- the Magic Kingdom to Epcot, for example -- you must place your finger on an electronic reader to gain admittance. Easy, right?

Not quite.

It turns out that not all of us have fingerprints. This may come as news to the F.B.I., which still uses fingerprints as a primary form of identification, but it wasn't news to me. I haven't had fingerprints for years -- and I knew exactly when and how I lost them.

It was Christmas, naturally -- the time of year when other people have visions of sugarplums dancing in their heads and I sleep with one eye open to see what fresh hell is about to drop down my chimney.

On the Christmas in question, around 1995, my college-age kids came to spend the day with me, accompanied by their respective significant others (who, I am happy to report, they eventually married.)

The day began in the kitchen, where Elisabeth and I were making -- what else -- that traditional Christmas staple, "Monkey Bread," which, as everybody knows, was named for the Christmas monkeys who assist Santa at the

North Pole.

(I just made that up, but I think it would make a great Disney movie. Note to Disney: call my agent.)

I don't know where I got the idea to make Monkey Bread because, looking back, I think the name is stupid. Is it named Monkey Bread because monkeys eat it? If so, I probably wouldn't like it, because I've seen other things monkeys eat and they certainly don't look that appetizing.

Maybe it means the bread is made out of monkey meat, in which case I absolutely don't want anything to do with it.

Somebody finally explained that the name comes from the way you are supposed to eat the bread -- like monkeys -- pulling off pieces and stuffing it into your mouth with your fingers.

In other words, the way we eat most everything.

I got the recipe from a magazine, I do remember that. It calls for three packages of refrigerated biscuit dough, two cups of sugar, a cup of butter, three tablespoons of cinnamon and a half cup each of raisins and chopped walnuts. What's not to like?

It requires a bundt cake pan -- a round pan with a hole in the middle -- which, I learned, is designed so that everything bakes evenly -- a process that, according to the directions, would take 32 minutes in a 350 degree oven, followed by a ten-minute cooling period. Then the pan was to be flipped upside down onto a serving plate.

That's when the problem started.

I should first mention that Elisabeth is extremely competent in the kitchen. She is also quick to volunteer to help out, and her energy and organizational skills make her a welcome assistant to any klutz in the kitchen --

namely, me. As an example, always protective of her old man, she solemnly advised me to wear oven mitts before reaching into the 350 degree oven to grab the pan.

Good call, I said, but I secretly wondered if she really thought I was dumb enough to grab a scorching hot pan without oven mitts.

It turns out I was.

When the bread came out of the oven, it smelled divine. I believe that something happens to cinnamon when it is heated -- something mysterious and scientific, resulting in such an odiferous explosion in your head that you momentarily lose all all your senses.

In other words, after I withdrew the pan from the oven with my oven-mitted hands, I turned it upside down onto a serving plate -- completely forgetting the ten minute "cooling" period -- and the bread began to overflow the plate, onto the counter. This is not necessarily a bad thing, as my kitchen counters are not subject to third-degree burns.

My hands, however, are.

Without a second thought, I grabbed the entire round loaf of sizzling hot sugary buttered bread with my now bare hands and, a microsecond later, dropped it in a heap onto the floor. My hands were now one with the bread, as it were -- at least the part of the bread that was still stuck to them, bubbling away as if still in the oven. I looked in horror at my daughter, who mirrored the same look back at me (times ten) and I saw that her mouth was open as in that Edvard Munch painting, *The Scream.*

The only difference between the Munch painting and my daughter was the addition of sound. Lots of it.

All of a sudden I wondered if my smoldering hands

were only the sign of a much bigger problem. Maybe my whole body was on fire. I briefly thought I should "drop and roll" -- as they teach you to do when you are on fire -- but I realized if I did, I'd be rolling around in the gurgling lava mess on the floor. I regained enough of my composure (the cinnamon smell had been replaced with the smell of burning flesh) to run to the sink and thrust my hands under water.

Elisabeth continued to scream as the neighbors no doubt raced to their windows to see where that noise was coming from. Meanwhile, the other three kids came running into the kitchen to see if I was dead.

My hands were eventually covered with some antibiotic cream and gauze, rendering them useless. For the rest of the day the kids amused themselves by taking turns shoveling food into my mouth, just like monkeys.

Meanwhile, my fingerprints had apparently burned completely off, so after the commotion at Disney dies down (caused by my lack of fingerprints) I plan to make a living by robbing banks.

Banana Bread I

If you ever receive a Christmas gift in the mail from me, you should probably open it with great care. Ideally, you would take it to the airport and run it through the x-ray machine. At the very least, if it says "Rex John" in the upper left corner, you should probably wear a bio-hazard suit when you open it.

More than a dozen of my friends learned this lesson the hard way years ago when, for the first (and last) time, I decided to make my own Christmas gifts.

This took place shortly after I arrived in Houston, and I was completely broke, due to my divorce and the cross-country move. Buying Christmas gifts wasn't in the budget, so I decided to use my many artistic talents to craft something for my closest friends.

That presented an immediate problem, since I don't have any artistic talent, and certainly nothing worth wrapping as a gift.

But that changed one day a month before Christmas when I was standing in the checkout at the grocery store.

Most of us browse the magazine covers as we wait for

the clerk to ring up our groceries, and this applies to men as well as women. How else would we learn of Kristen Stewart's "Boob Job Shocker!" or the inside story of the "World's Fattest Bride"? If I hadn't been looking at those magazine covers that chilly November day, I might not have seen an article entitled "What Gourmet Cooks are Making This Christmas."

That's all I needed to know. I tossed the magazine into my cart and I knew my problem was solved. All I needed to do was become a gourmet cook and then whip something up to mail to my friends.

This wasn't an original idea. In fact, I can remember being the recipient of food gifts on many occasions, the first when I was in junior high school and Mrs. Lerner, our next-door neighbor, brought over a covered potato and noodle casserole called "Kugel" as a little Hanukkah gift. Apparently the Santa and reindeer on the roof and the nativity scene in the yard hadn't registered on her, and she swore she thought we were Jewish. My mother, who drove up the driveway just as Mrs. Lerner rang the doorbell, intercepted her on the porch and commenced arguing with her that "she really shouldn't have," and so on, but as they bickered, the greasy kugel dripped all over, leaving big, oily stains that are there to this day.

One of my grandmothers also enjoyed giving food gifts, and each year she made peanut brittle for everyone in the family. If you think that peanut brittle is a good gift, you must be a dentist.

The more I thought about the idea of making an edible gift, the more I liked it. No more fighting the crowds at Saks and Tiffany's! From now on, I'd just breeze through the check-out at Safeway and Piggly Wiggly. As a bonus I could peruse the magazines.

It didn't take long before I encountered my first problem: I don't cook.

Not to be dissuaded, I read the magazine carefully and familiarized myself with what the other gourmet cooks would be making for their friends.

One recipe sounded unique, which is always good for Christmas gifts. It was "Christmas Oyster Stew," but I realized it might not be easy to ship, and I didn't know where to find "Christmas oysters."

"Curried Herring on Rye Toast" also sounded good but, again, I decided transport might be an issue.

I tossed the magazine and turned to my cookbook shelf.

Calling a bookshelf a "cookbook shelf" is somewhat grandiose, given the fact that it held precisely two never-used cookbooks and a framed photo of my kids in which they looked hungry and bored. I guess the photo was intended to motivate me to learn how to cook, but it didn't. I eventually replaced it with a photo of the three of us eating in a restaurant.

Curiously, I discovered that my name actually appeared in one of the two cookbooks, a cute little spiral bound book entitled, "Kids' Favorite Recipes." The only reason my name appeared in the acknowledgements was because I was on the board of directors of Adopt-a-School, the organization that printed it. As I recall, it was created as a fundraising project.

After a while, in perusing the table of contents, I saw that one of the recipes was for a peanut butter and jelly sandwich, so I was pretty sure I could handle the skill level required.

I ended up choosing a recipe called "Banana Bread I."

There was also a "Banana Bread II," but that sounded too advanced.

I made my shopping list, which was substantial, as I needed to make sixteen loaves of Banana Bread I. When I got the stuff home, I set out the ingredients on the kitchen table and wondered briefly if I could make the whole thing at once. That didn't seem feasible, since I didn't have a bowl quite big enough to hold 16 eggs, 24 cups of flour and 64 ripened bananas. *Sixty-four!* Nor did I have sixteen loaf pans. So, I decided to work in batches.

The process of banana bread-making isn't interesting enough to repeat here, but suffice it to say the kitchen took a major hit.

When I was finished, I stood proud and tall, like other accomplished chefs -- Chef Boyardee comes to mind. There, before me, were sixteen lovely, plump, fragrant loaves of bread. They filled every inch of the countertop. I'd deliberately made two extra loaves -- one for me "just to make sure it tastes okay" -- and one for the kids on Christmas morning. I remember that it was about two o'clock in the morning when I cut into my first slice of Banana Bread I.

It was sublime.

What a hit my gifts would be!

The following day I prepared them for mailing. This really would be a first -- it was still at least a month before Christmas, which left plenty of time to carefully wrap and ship them to arrive before the 25th.

First I wrapped each loaf in plastic wrap, and then aluminum foil, to ensure freshness. Next I wrapped each one in tissue paper and put it in a loaf-sized gift box, purchased specially for the project. I wrapped each box with Christmas paper and added a bow and a handwritten card. They were then placed in mailing cartons, and "Do Not Open 'til Christmas" labels affixed. This done, I hauled all of them -- except the two I'd reserved -- to the post office. I wrapped one of the reserves just like the others -- and put it under our tree.

Going to the post office is always fun. Best of all, since the most I could carry at once was six loaves, I got to go through the line three times!

It took all morning.

This (monumental) task complete, all I had to do was sit back and wait for the accolades to roll in.

Meanwhile, I finished that first loaf (net weight gain: two pounds) and continued to keep my eye on the one under the tree, trying at various times to justify eating it myself on the grounds that "the kids probably wouldn't like it anyway." But, for once, discipline won out and it was still there on Christmas morn.

Like a bomb waiting to go off.

I wasn't with any of the recipients on Christmas morning, so I wasn't able to see the look of joy that surely filled their faces -- but, strangely, not one of them sent me a thank-you note.

I do know about the look that filled my face, however.

In my ongoing desire that my kids not turn out like those pushy/greedy/grabby children who tear through their gifts on Christmas morning, I suggested that we have "a little treat" before we started opening gifts. I won't say they were ecstatic with that idea, but they went along with it. I poured myself a cup of coffee and each of them a glass of juice before asking Elisabeth to open the box that I knew held the banana bread. I waited expectantly as the wrapping paper came off.

My first hint that something wasn't quite right was when Elisabeth gasped and ran to the bathroom. Jonathan looked inside the box and said, "Ewwwww..." before tossing the whole thing into my lap.

Inside was a living, breathing organism -- a solid block of mold of such a dark, rich color that at first I wondered if the loaf had somehow transformed itself into a brown hedgehog or some other furry animal.

All that was missing was a petrie dish and Madame Curie.

"Will it bite?" Jonathan asked sarcastically.

I quietly excused myself and went to the kitchen for rubber gloves. Holding the box gingerly, lest it escape and run wild through the house, I walked all the way out to the dumpster and threw it in with a resounding thud before securing the lid tightly. I prayed that some stray animal wouldn't get hold of it and die -- possibly starting a new epidemic disease.

Returning to the living room, where the kids sat ashen-faced, gifts unopened, it still hadn't registered on me that at least fourteen other people were having the same wonderful experience in their own living rooms that Christmas morning -- which may explain why I didn't receive any thank-you notes.

That evening, neighborhood carolers stood on our porch singing a medley of Christmas songs. The three of us listened from the doorway as they sang all two hundred and thirty-seven verses of "The Twelve Days of Christmas," with its endless list of maids-a-milking, turtle doves, geese a-laying, leaping lords, etc., etc.

The only thing it seems his true love *didn't* send was a

moldy loaf of Banana Bread I.

Applesauce and the Fine Art of Decorating

The other day Brad asked me to purchase some applesauce when I went to the market. Instead, I went running to Google to look for assisted living facilities, since I consider a request for applesauce to be one step away from wearing adult diapers.

My stepmother, who lived to be 94, ate applesauce every day of her adult life. Moreover, she ate it three times a day: for breakfast she had eggs, bacon, toast and applesauce. For lunch she had a grilled cheese sandwich and applesauce. For dinner she had a microwaved meal accompanied by applesauce. Believe it or not, this was her choice, and I permitted it since she was an adult and could do, as she so sweetly put it, whatever she damn well pleased.

But since I equate eating applesauce with growing old, I began watching Brad closely for other telltale signs -- like wearing dentures and using a walker. He makes this difficult, however. Dentures are out because he flosses his teeth forty-nine times a day and could probably chew a tree down. A walker? That's out, too. He bicycles about

50 miles a day, up and down mountain roads that would exhaust me just driving them in a car.

So, I bought the applesauce.

I don't like to admit it, but my stepmother may have been on to something. She didn't see a doctor for the last forty years of her life -- until she fell on two occasions and had to be briefly hospitalized. She didn't take any medications, except applesauce and large quantities of alcohol. In fact, in my opinion she would probably be alive today, were it not for the fact that the second time she fell she broke her arm and developed an infection.

That's not to say she was a specimen of good mental health. She didn't leave her house for the last ten years of her life, afraid to go as far as her patio for fear she would fall. Nothing I could say would convince her that she was safe -- even though I offered to hold her tightly with each step.

I noted her bizarre behavior when I traveled home to see her about four years before she died. I thought it would be a quick visit: in and out of town over a long weekend, but as soon as I arrived I realized it wouldn't be that easy. In the six months since my last visit, she had grown frail. She now needed somebody to help her, and unfortunately there wasn't anybody to do it but me. So, I moved back home -- after a forty-plus year absence -- and became, for two years, her full-time caregiver.

There are no funny stories to be told of that difficult time. I watched as this fiercely independent woman became more and more dependent upon me. For years she said that her greatest fear was being forced into a "nursing home," and I had foolishly promised that I would never allow that to happen. But that was then.

When faced with no alternatives, those promises came back to bite me in the you-know-what. Still, I was resolved to keep it from happening for as long as possible.

After two years, I knew I couldn't take it another minute. I did love her -- she was the only mother I knew from the age of eleven onward, and I wanted what any son wants for his mother: for her to be happy and feel loved in her old age.

But enough was enough.

I am not cut out for caregiving. It's just not in my DNA. When I finally realized that being a full-time caregiver was more than I could handle, I sat down and gently broached the forbidden subject with her.

"Mother," I said, "you know that it has been two years since I came home to take care of you..."

"Yes, I know," she said. "And I appreciate it so much..."

"Yes, well. The fact is, I don't think I can do it anymore -- and I'm so sorry, but I think we need to find a better living arrangement for both of us."

"That's fine, Rex," she said. "You do what you need to do. But I'll be staying right here..."

"No, Mother. That's simply not possible. Look at all the things I do for you. You could never take care of this big house by yourself."

"Oh yes I can. Who do you think did it before you came home?"

"I know," I said. "But that was then, when you had more strength...when you could actually walk up and down the stairs...or get up by yourself in the middle of the night..."

"Well, I'm not going anywhere," she said, and there

was a chilling finality in the words.

And she didn't.

I felt she was being selfish, and told her so. It didn't make any difference. In frustration, I phoned my kids to vent. "Your Grandmother," I said, the exasperation showing in my voice, "refuses to budge out of this house, but there's no way she can continue living here by herself."

Hearing myself, my brain fast-forwarded to how I might behave when I am Mother's age. I am every bit as capable of being stubborn as she is; what if I dug in my heels and refused to be reasonable about my daily care? I couldn't -- wouldn't -- do to my kids what I thought Mother was doing to me. "So," I said, "Let me tell you something. When you think it's time to put *me* in an assisted living facility, I am giving you permission right now to do it. You don't have to ask me, and you shouldn't listen to me if I balk. Just do it. When you think it's time, just do it!"

My son, without missing a beat said, "I think it's time."

After hiring caregivers to stay with her 7 days a week, I moved out. It cost a fortune, but it enabled me to slowly recover my sanity, and it allowed her to remain in the home she loved so much.

Mother died a year later, and it became my responsibility to prepare the house for sale. Brad painted it inside and out and fixed up the yard: planting flowers, trimming bushes and trees and moving the hose around all day long so the lawn wouldn't die.

We both cleaned carpets and floors and emptied out the basement of some forty years of accumulated stuff, including every plastic butter tub that ever came through the door. We had two garage sales, and I saw first hand that it is true that "one man's trash is another man's treasure." That, and the fact that people have terrible taste. Nothing underscored this fact more than the sale of three "paintings" I had done years earlier, when I lived in Houston.

I had attended a gallery reception in which abstract paintings were being sold for five and six figures. I examined the pieces carefully -- from up close and from afar, and for the life of me I couldn't see how they justified their exorbitant prices. I needed some large pieces for my own walls at home, but there was no way I could afford any of the art I saw in the gallery. So, I decided I would just have to make my own. The next day, I bought three large canvases and some primary colors. How hard could it be to paint geometric shapes?

Let's just say it's harder than you might think. But, eventually, I managed to get a square, circle and triangle onto the three canvases, and I hung them on the walls of my living room just to see how my friends would mock me.

Some did, but I didn't care: I knew they were awful, but I kept them up because they covered otherwise bare walls.

When I moved back home to care for Mother, the paintings came with me, simply because they were so big I wasn't sure how to dispose of them. I put them on the naked concrete walls in the basement and forgot all about them.

When the house went up for sale, we received several offers and, of course, accepted the best one. The only condition the prospective buyer had was that the three paintings in the basement be included! I could barely suppress my laughter. Not only did I no longer have to worry about how to dispose of them, I was, in effect, getting paid to do so!

The house looked good when we sold it. It is said that all gay men are born with the ability to arrange flowers, understand fashion and transform drab spaces into showplaces. I don't quite fit the profile. My idea of arranging flowers is to cut them all the same length and shove them in a vase. If I'm feeling particularly daring I'll dump in that little envelope of cocaine that comes from the florist to make the blooms last longer.

And, as I have already mentioned, I think any male who has worn, at various times, a dress, a Ben Casey doctor shirt, and a synthetic fur coat is immediately disqualified as a fashion expert.

Thus, if I am to be certified as a gay man, that leaves only interior design: the "ability to transform drab spaces."

My childhood home certainly qualified as a drab space.

Built in the early 60s, after my dad remarried, our new house was everything a kid could hope for at the time. My dad was a building contractor, so of course it was all done to his exacting standards, as at least a half-dozen workers who were fired during its construction can attest.

One of my favorite features of that house was the built in intercom/a.m. radio system, which was a novelty in those days. I could invite my friends over and station them in various rooms of the house and then broadcast witty remarks to wherever they were, simply by flipping certain switches. But since I didn't have that many friends, I had to play with the system by myself. When I came home to an empty house after school (which was most of the time) I operated the master control like a rocket launch station, a police command center or a radio station. Lowering my voice to sound like a radio announcer, I would flip the buttons to send my message to whichever room I had designated and then I would run to that room to listen for my own voice. The fact that to do so would require breaking the sound barrier was lost on me. But even though this little game never worked as intended, I pretended it did and, flipping the switch at the remote station, I would issue a snappy reply before running back to the master control in the kitchen to hear what I said.

Okay, so I was delusional.

Sometimes I would play the role of a spy, listening intently to what I imagined was heavy breathing coming from one of the bedrooms before surprising the make-believe couple by screaming into the microphone, "I can hear you, you know! And I know you're having sex! Stop that! Stop that right now!" Then I laughed as only an 11-year old can laugh, because I barely knew what sex was, much less how it worked. That particular broadcast was one of my favorites until I accidentally sent it bellowing out to the front porch a split second before a male/female couple of Jehovah's Witnesses rang the bell. I don't know who was more embarrassed when I opened the front door.

Our house also had one of the few swimming pools in town. When it was being built, the country had just come through the Cuban missile crisis, so Dad wasn't taking any chances. He increased the size of the underground pool equipment room by fifty square feet and installed a bomb-proof steel door. He told us the space would double as a bomb shelter in the case of a nuclear incident. I didn't have the nerve to point out that breathing might prove difficult, since we also stored chlorine in that space. Besides, I knew that the only way to survive a nuclear disaster was to take cover under your desk.

Even then my parents and I had wildly divergent taste in furnishings. I wanted things that were stylish and up-to-date, whereas they, in my opinion, wanted crap. And since they were paying for it, you can guess what we got: Danish modern crap.

The family room in that house was my least favorite, because it contained a Danish-modern sofa, a Danish-modern coffee table, a Danish-modern television console and two of the biggest, ugliest Barcaloungers ever made. And because neither of my parents ever left those chairs once they settled into them for the evening -- every evening, seven days a week -- the chairs looked pretty raggedy after a year. After two years, they were ready for the dump.

Unfortunately they were still there, in the same spot, when I arrived home some forty years later. I knew I would be well on my way to becoming a world-famous interior designer if I just got rid of those chairs. So I did.

I also got rid of every stick of furniture, half the walls, the carpet that had lasted ten years but been kept for forty, all the polyester draperies, the kitchen cabinets and countertops, and the yellow toilet in the guest bathroom -- an unfortunate color choice, since you could never tell if you had peed or not.

A few years later, Brad and I finished fixing up the house and put it on the market, it sold quickly, even in the midst of a terrible real estate market. I was proud of us until Brad, who keeps track of this sort of thing, told me we could have sold the house without fixing it up and come out $50,000 ahead.

"Not a problem," I said. "Let's pretend it didn't happen and start all over again."

This line of reasoning ("Rex Logic" he calls it) baffles him, but I remind him that at least I am consistent. Following the sale of Mother's house, we bought another house, which resulted in a $12,000 loss. After that, we bought another (we were getting experience, I reminded him) which resulted in a $10,000 loss.

"See?" I told him. "We're getting better!"

I recently saw a house listed nearby which would be an excellent candidate for a "fix-n-flip," but for some reason he doesn't seem that interested.

Gary, Is That You?

I've always been a sucker for rags-to-riches stories, although my own trajectory has been somewhat the opposite. In truth, I like any tale in which something changes. I tire quickly of the status quo. This may be explained by my astrological sign.

Actually, I'm not a big believer in astrology. I don't know much about it -- except my own sign: Gemini. Geminis, I am told, don't like to be bored. This quality -- along with the fact that Geminis supposedly have dual personalities -- makes me think there may be something to it after all.

My grandmother once told me that one of my earliest utterances was the phrase, "I'm bored" -- except the word "bored" was drawn out to a long whine: *"I'm borrrrrrrrrrrred...."*

Today I'd probably be diagnosed as having attention deficit disorder, and I would be given a big dose of Ritalin which would enable me, among other things, to perform complicated mathematical equations, like multiplying numbers by 8 or 9.

I would love to have the laser focus that Brad does. To call it "focus" is an understatement. I'll bet he could burn a hole through paper just by staring at it.

I don't have focus. I am attracted to shiny objects or movement of any kind. A ceiling fan can keep me occupied for hours.

Anything in flight also works.

We have hummingbirds on our patio in Palm Springs, and I love it when one of them comes within an inch of my face, fluttering its little wings at 50 beats per *second*. We were sitting outside one sunny morning when this happened and I whispered to Brad, "Look!" so he could see this frenetic little bird only inches in front of me.

"He's probably getting ready to drill into your eyeball for nectar," he said.

I shooed him away. The bird, too.

This particular hummingbird has a name: Gary. The name was bestowed on him by one of our best friends in honor of her deceased husband whose name was also -- well, Gary. I found out about this one day when she and I were standing on her patio down the street and a hummingbird buzzed us. "Oh look," she exclaimed. "It's Gary!"

This puzzled me, because for a moment I thought she might be seeing an apparition and I wanted to see it too, because I've been very cranky with God lately about what's going on in the world and I've been hoping someone would deliver a message to Him for me.

When I realized she was talking about the hummingbird, I tried to put on my best "I hope you're not crazy" face and said, eyebrows arched, "Gary?"

"Yes," she explained. "Gary loved hummingbirds, so

I'll bet this is Gary coming back to see us." That would have been enough, but at that point she called out to the hummingbird in a sing-song voice, "Hi, Gary! Hi, Gary!" and, curiously, the hummingbird seemed to do an about-face as if to say, "You talkin' to me?"

So now Brad and I refer to every hummingbird who comes near us as "Gary," and we greet them all by calling out a friendly greeting: "Hi, Gary!"

In other words, we're as crazy as she is.

Dinner is Served

Being easily bored as a child is one thing -- a nearby adult can simply spin you in circles until you get dizzy and pass out, or they can throw a book at you and order you to read it. But as an adult, it's more complicated.

I had a moment of unplanned brilliance when I decided to start my own public relations firm. Starting my own business meant that unlike all the jobs I had had up until that point, if I got tired of what I was doing, I could just find a new client and work on their stuff for a while.

But after twenty years, boredom struck again, and even new clients didn't do it for me.

That's about the time Brad and I finished fixing up Mother's old house for sale and, based on the fact that we had a lot of fun doing it, we decided to enter the wonderful world of house-flipping.

To prepare ourselves, we watched TV. Well, I watched TV; Brad read books. He familiarized himself with the intricacies of buying a suitable property based on an accurate assessment of its strengths and weaknesses given current market indicators, the age and condition of the property, the suitability and sell-ability of the neighborhood, and so forth.

Yawn.

I simply found programs on A&E and HGTV that featured investors who bought crappy old properties and fixed them up for practically nothing before selling them for a fortune. How complicated is that?

Unfortunately, I didn't pay attention to the copyright date of the programs I was watching and, as it turns out, most of them were made around MMIV -- according to the credits that run at warp-speed at the end of each program.

For those who don't speak Latin as a second language, MMIV is the year 2004 and that was three full years before the big real estate crash of MMVII (2007). We started our "flipping" business (in every sense of the word) two years later, in MMIX (2009).

One thing I learned from watching HGTV is that I don't like it that they use Roman numerals for the copyright date. Apparently they haven't noticed that we no longer speak Latin in this country -- and, with the exception of Miss Archibald, my high school Latin teacher, *non puto unquam.* (I don't think we ever did.)

The other thing I learned -- the hard way -- was that all the so-called profits from house-flipping had long ago disappeared into the pockets of the banks and mortgage companies.

That's not to say we weren't cautious, even though all the data from which we were operating was now invalid. True to form, Brad researched dozens if not hundreds of potential properties before deciding on two or three that we went to see in person.

I wanted to buy every house we drove past, whether it was for sale or not. "There! That one! Or that one! How about that one!" Reason prevailed, thank goodness, and every offer we made fell through because Brad refused to pay twice as much as we should have. Spoil sport.

Eventually I found a house he couldn't say "no" to. A friend of ours had lost her job and was about to lose her house. If I'd had the money, I would have bought it and given it to her as a gift, but since I'm not Richie Rich, I couldn't do that. But the least we could do, I told Brad, was buy her house so she wouldn't lose it to foreclosure and destroy her otherwise perfect credit record. I came up with what I thought was a noble plan: we would buy her house for what she owed the bank, then we would fix it up with our money before selling it and dividing the profit between her and us. I was so proud of this generous impulse that we almost had trouble getting my head through the door to look at the place.

Our friend was so grateful that she wrote us at least a hundred thank-you notes -- or so it seemed. She moved into a smaller rental property and we were suddenly the proud new owners of a lovely two bedroom, two bathroom condominium on the top floor of a high rise building in a tony section of Denver. How could we possibly lose?

Other than normal wear and tear to be expected with an older property, it was in decent shape, but its best feature, in addition to the neighborhood in which it was located, was its stunning views of the Colorado rockies and the downtown skyline.

Our only surprise came the day we tried to ensure that

the fireplace was in working order. Denver doesn't permit fireplace fires, yet the building department still requires that they be certified as operable. They seem to be saying "you absolutely cannot have a fireplace, but if you do, it must work properly."

Normally, I would categorize chimney cleaning as a "Brad job," since all Rex jobs involve pushing a button and allowing a machine to do the work (e.g., washing the dishes and doing the laundry) -- or hiring a maid. But when I tried to get Brad to clean the chimney, he wouldn't touch it with a ten-foot pole (or even a ten-foot chimney brush.) So we hired it out.

Chimney sweeps, it turns out, aren't just a figure of Mary Poppins's dreams. They still exist, and not just in Merry Olde England -- and they ain't that bad looking, either. The one who came to sweep our chimney could have moonlighted as a male model (after he cleaned up a bit, that is.)

Before he arrived, I had been whining about how hungry I was -- it was about four o'clock in the afternoon -- and I couldn't stop talking about various things that sounded good to eat. But when Chimney Jimney showed up, all thoughts of food were temporarily put aside.

He, in his white shirt and tight jeans, went about preparing the room -- putting drop cloths all over the furniture and floors -- and then asked where the roof was.

"Ummm...upstairs?" I ventured.

I said he was good looking, not brilliant.

While he went up to the roof I knelt expectantly in front of the fireplace like a kid expecting to catch Santa arriving any minute. Never mind that it was July.

Sure enough, it wasn't long before "I heard on the roof

the prancing and pawing of each little hoof...as I drew in my head, and was turning around, down the chimney St. Nicholas came with a bound!" Only it wasn't St. Nicholas that came plopping at my feet.

It was a pigeon.

I didn't need to perform an autopsy to see that this particular pigeon had been dead and slow roasted for who-knows-how long.

Brad, who had wandered into another room once the chimney sweep went up on the roof, came back in just as the pigeon fell out of the fireplace and landed at my feet.

He took one look at it. "Dinner!" he said.

Nature. You Can Have It.

My definition of irony is being seated in the first class cabin of an international flight -- with Africa as the final destination.

The part I like is first class travel -- especially when someone else is paying for it -- which is exactly what happened to me a few years ago when my friends Greg and John invited me to go with them to South Africa for a few days. Greg was in medical school and working for an airline at the time, and because he could fly for free, it wasn't uncommon for him to go halfway around the world for a long weekend.

Generally, I like to see new places. Who can forget the first time they saw New York, Chicago, San Francisco, Paris, or London? These are wonderful places and they all have one thing in common: they're not in Africa.

New York, for example, has Bloomingdales and the Plaza Hotel.

Chicago has the Magnificent Mile, Second City and the Peninsula.

San Francisco has the Golden Gate, cable cars and the

Mark Hopkins.

Paris has the Musée d'Orsay, Angelina Chocolates and the Ritz.

London has Westminster Abbey, Buckingham Palace and the London Bridge. (Well, actually, the London Bridge is now located in Lake Havasu City, Arizona, but so far Westminster Abbey and Buckingham Palace have stayed put.) It also has the Connaught Hotel.

Africa, on the other hand, has wild animals that will hunt you down and eat you, snakes that can swallow you whole, and spiders that lay eggs in your ears at night and lodge in trees where only cheetahs can climb.

Have I made my point?

John and Greg told me I was mistaken. They said that may be true in the "outer" regions of Africa, but we would be going to *South* Africa. "Oh," I snorted. "You mean like the *South* Bronx or *South* L.A.?"

"No," Greg said. "Cape Town is one of the most beautiful cities in the world and it really is a city -- with skyscrapers and everything."

"Oh, really?" I said. "How do you define a skyscraper?"

"I don't know…," Greg said, with some annoyance. "At least 20 floors."

"Ha!" I said. "The Empire State Building has 102 floors." But I had to admit it: I was intrigued. I had no idea there was anything more than game parks in Africa.

"*South* Africa," Greg corrected once again. "Cape Town is located in *South* Africa. There's a difference. Cape Town is a real city, with real hotels and great wineries. Plus," he added, "I got us first class tickets."

That's all I needed to hear.

Nobody likes flying any more. It is rude and uncomfortable. For me, the worst part is sitting in one of those dinky coach-class seats for two or three hours, fighting for a sliver of armrest and aiming the air nozzle at your neighbor so your own eyeballs won't get so dry that you can no longer blink.

Two or three hours is one thing, but thirty-two hours -- the flight time from Houston to Cape Town -- is quite another. I can't imagine how painful it would be back in coach.

As it turned out, I didn't need to imagine it, because Greg's partner John was seated in coach, and he was happy to tell us all about it.

Don't ask me why we were in front and John was in back -- all I know is when we tried to sneak John into an unused seat across the aisle from us, the flight attendant sent him packing.

So, while Greg and I occupied ourselves by trying to make our toes reach the end of the electric footrests, John got to sit in a coach class seat with his legs wrapped around his own neck.

Fortunately, he had superb in-flight cuisine to take his mind off the uncomfortable seats. Not the cuisine served in coach, of course -- I'm sure that was half an old sandwich or something -- but, rather, the food we were served in first class, which Greg dutifully went back and described to John periodically during the flight.

Frankly, I'm surprised Greg didn't end up in the overhead compartment with a first-class pillow stuffed in his mouth.

When we arrived in Cape Town, I had to admit that Greg had told the truth about the place. It is a beautiful, cosmopolitan city, with lovely tree-lined streets, the magnificent Cape itself, and a sprinkling of five-star hotels -- not that we stayed in one.

Greg, who is, shall we say, "careful" with money, arranged for us to stay in an inexpensive Bed and Breakfast owned and operated by a big-boned German woman named Frau Krueger. Let's just say Frau Krueger probably isn't known for her looks.

I soon discovered that Frau Krueger had what some people refer to as "German sensibilities about matters of comfort." Translation: she's a tightwad.

When she showed me to my room, I asked if I could have a blanket. "Vye do you need blanket?" she asked, incredulously. "Colt air is goot for you!"

John and I flashed a knowing look at each other. There was actually somebody cheaper than Greg -- and he had managed to find her!

This was confirmed to us the next morning. When we filed into the dining room at exactly seven o'clock -- as we had been ordered to do the night before -- it was so early the sun hadn't even come up. The only light in the room came from the pre-dawn glimmer sifting through the white lace curtains. We could hardly make out the furniture, so John thoughtfully flipped the switch for the overhead light, instantly bathing the room in a romantic glow as only a 25-watt bulb can do. At least we could now make out each other's faces.

We sat down, but apparently Frau Krueger had seen the burst of 25-watt light and came flying out of the kitchen to find out who was wasting all that electricity.

John admitted that he was the one who had flipped the switch, so she came over and thwacked him on the back of the head -- something they rarely do at the Ritz-Carlton. "Vhat's wrong wit you!" she said. "Ve don't need lights on in the middle of the day!" It was now 7:15.

Apparently she didn't believe in leaving the porch light on, either, because during the night our rental car was broken into and our car stereo ripped right out of the dashboard.

"Nice neighborhood, Greg," John said.

We picked up the broken glass -- the thief apparently used a wing window in the back seat to gain entry -- but we decided not to have it fixed, since we would only be there for a few more days.

Our first destination was a drive around the Cape of Good Hope -- or, as I learned to call it, the "Cape of I Hope The Baboons Don't Kill Us."

As we set out on our journey, John, who had been studying the guide books, said, "Oh! They have penguins here! Let's go see the penguins!"

This made me feel uneasy. I've spent some time with penguins, and I'm not that crazy about them. In 1988 I was in San Diego to attend the Super Bowl, because the Denver Broncos were playing. During the week leading up to the game I was assigned as a PR flak for the Governor of Colorado and the Mayor of Denver, both of whom were in California to support our home team.

When doing PR for politicians, one quickly learns that it is one photo-op after another. One such event was scheduled at Sea World, one of San Diego's foremost attractions -- and where they had just opened a new penguin exhibit. I didn't make the arrangements, so I never figured out how the Governor of Colorado and the Mayor of Denver would benefit from seeing penguins in

San Diego, but it wasn't my job to reason why. With newspaper and TV reporters in tow, we made the visit.

We ambled though the park where we eventually came upon a large, glassed-in enclosure in which thirty or forty penguins seemed to be wandering around trying to figure out why they were thusly imprisoned. We stood looking through the glass, nodding appreciatively as park officials told us everything anybody ever wanted to know about penguins. "Any questions?" our cheerful young escort asked at the end of her lecture.

"What do they taste like?" I wanted to ask her, but I thought better of it.

She then invited us to go inside the enclosure -- with the actual penguins. The politicians, sensing a photo-op if ever there was one, jumped at the offer. I, on the other hand, was less enthusiastic. The thought of getting close to these slimy-looking creatures didn't appeal to me.

But before I knew it, the three of us -- the Governor, the Mayor and I -- were given heavy parkas (it was plenty hot on that particular day in San Diego, so that alone was a special treat) and then, in what should have been a big clue as to what came next, we were given big rubber boots to wear.

After being ushered inside the sub-zero enclosure which, I assume, is not unlike getting inside one's own freezer -- if your freezer were full of penguin poop, that is -- the reason for the boots became clear. As if on cue, the penguins began coming up to us and leaving little penguin poop welcome gifts at our feet. (For the record, I prefer a glass of champagne.) We had been given a pail of fish as we walked in ("Thanks, but I just ate lunch...,") which the Governor and the Mayor promptly passed to me and I passed back to the park personnel who were accompanying us. The employees then tossed fish around which created a minor stir -- and more penguin deposits on our rubber boots.

The thing I remember best is not their cute little faces, but the fact that it smelled like fish guts and penguin poop in there. It was like being trapped in an outhouse. A penguin outhouse.

So, while John and Greg were excited about seeing the penguins in Cape Town, I was less than enthusiastic -- especially when I discovered that this wasn't just another penguin enclosure like the one at Sea World -- but simply a big beach *out in the open* with thousands of penguins running around making a noise that can only be described as hee-haw -- the same noise a donkey makes. Hee-haw, hee-haw -- times a million.

Where are all the penguin-eating orca whales when you need them?

Thankfully, Greg and John soon decided they had seen enough penguins. It was time to get back in the car and continue down the highway toward Table Mountain National Park -- via the Cape of I Hope The Baboons Don't Kill Us.

Everybody knows about the baboons in South Africa. Also the lions, tigers, elephants, giraffes -- the whole circus. That's why I took special pains to exact a promise from Greg and John that we wouldn't be going outside the city limits -- much less on a "safari."

I should have been more specific. Table Mountain Park is just like a city zoo, easily located within the city limits. But, unlike most zoos, this one doesn't have cages. It's one big cage, and you're in it -- along with the wild animals.

After driving along for half an hour without spotting man nor beast, all of a sudden we were in a traffic jam. We stopped at the end of the line of cars and waited for traffic to resume. But then the occupants of the car in front of us began to climb out as though they might just leave it in the middle of the road and go for a stroll in the woods. Then we saw that other people were getting out of their cars, too. I was about the open my door -- I was sitting in the back seat -- and go see what was happening when, without warning, everybody began screaming and running back to their cars.

"What's going on?" I asked.

"Oh, I think it's probably just baboons," Greg said.

"Baboons?" I said, trying to match his nonchalance, as though spotting baboons in the middle of the highway was an everyday occurrence. (Brad: "How was the traffic in downtown Denver today?" Me: "Oh, it was fine....you know, a few snarls, a couple of accidents and, oh, half a dozen baboons sitting around in the middle of I-25...")

"Yes," Greg said, becoming more excited. "Maybe one of them will come over to the car!"

"You mean to wash our windshield?" I asked.

"No, stupid. To beg for food."

"Well," I said as I began searching the back seat, "I don't think we have any."

"Oh no!" he exclaimed. "We can't feed them, no matter what. If we do, they'll never leave. That's why there are signs every twenty feet saying DO NOT FEED THE BABOONS."

"And," he added. "Whatever you do...,don't roll down your window -- even a crack, because they know how to unlock the door, and then they get inside and tear the car to pieces. They can be very aggressive."

"Right...," I said, but then I stopped talking because I spotted a big lumbering beast walking toward our car. For a split second I actually wondered if it was a guy wearing a gorilla suit. It wasn't.

He came up to John's window and looked at John as though they'd gone to school together. His buddy soon joined him and jumped onto the hood of our car, giving us an unobstructed view of all his baboon charms -- including those that should have been in some baboon underpants. Greg and John were laughing -- which I thought was rude, and so did the baboon, because he then started playing with himself.

I couldn't look. It seemed like a private moment between him and, well, Greg and John. So I looked down -- but turned my head when I detected movement beside me: a long, hairy arm slithering along the inside of the door, feeling for the handle.

I remember thinking, "Who are these creatures, and how do they know so much about the design of an automobile?"

It didn't take me long to figure out that I did not want him to find whatever he was feeling for. Instinctively, I threw myself back on the seat and thrust my feet at the hairy arm, kicking it away. It withdrew the same way it came in: through the small wing window which had been broken the night before. But it was a ploy. I could see that he was poised outside and preparing to slip his stinky arm through the hole again. I slammed my two feet against the opening. To get in, he would need to move my feet -- or tickle them. I'm very ticklish.

So I kept my feet anchored against the window -- or where the window should have been -- and shouted, "Oh. No. You. Don't!" -- hoping he understood English. This caused Greg and John, who were still mesmerized by the performance before them to turn around and ask, "What's going on?"

"This crazy baboon is trying to get in here, and now he's tapping on the bottom of my sneakers!"

Fortunately, the car behind us sensed that something bad was happening and began to back up.

"Get us out of here!" I screamed at Greg, who threw the car into reverse, causing the baboon on the hood to roll off like a big hairy bowling ball. But he landed on his feet and I wondered if he was going to throw his arms in the air like an Olympic gymnast.

Greg finally managed to maneuver the car into another lane and then aimed for the front of the line like foreigners at Disney World do.

But this didn't work. We came upon a large group of baboons who were clearly in no hurry to move. They were lounging in the middle of the highway like it was Occupy Wall Street. Greg laid on the horn and kept edging forward, and the honking eventually annoyed them enough that they got up and ambled out of the way.

We returned to our B&B, where the only thing we needed to worry about was using too much electricity.

Dame Penelope

"Penelope Parker is a silly old cow."

My co-worker Farhad is speaking, so I am only half-listening. Farhad is Iranian and doesn't like British people. Mrs. Parker is British.

Farhad claims to be related to the former Shah of Iran, and maybe he is, just like I'm related to Davy Crockett and Mary Queen of Scots.

Whether I listen to Farhad or not doesn't seem to deter him, so the fact that I'm only half-listening doesn't slow him down in the least as he continues his rant about Mrs. Parker -- or Dame Penelope as we sometimes called her. When Penelope stormed out of our office only a few minutes earlier she shouted over her shoulder, "Well, this will be the last you hear of me!"

Yeah, right.

As soon as the door slammed, Farhad started in, and I silently returned to the question I grapple with every Saturday afternoon: what am I doing here? This wasn't my regular job, thank goodness, but simply one of those things we all get roped into from time to time.

"Remember that time I helped you fix a flat tire? Well, it's payback time, dude. You need to help me move my furniture up four flights of stairs." That sort of thing. Stuff we would ordinarily never agree to, but because we owe a favor to the person who's asking, we feel we have no choice but to say yes.

So that's why I was working in the leasing office of my apartment complex on a hot Saturday afternoon -- and why I would be back again for each of the following eight Saturdays. The manager of the apartment complex, Gretchen, had once done me a favor, and now it was my turn to do something nice for her.

"I can only visit my daughter on weekends," she told me, "so is there any chance you could cover for me?"

Sensing my hesitation, she tried to reassure me. "It will be easy," she said. "Farhad will be here with you, and all you need to do is greet prospective tenants and give Farhad a bathroom break once in awhile."

Giving Farhad a bathroom break was just too enticing and I could imagine the entry on my resume. "Considerable experience in providing relief to those in need."

When Gretchen told me that Saturdays were the only days to visit her daughter, I assumed her daughter might be sick or even dying.

"Don't be stupid," Farhad said when I put forth this hypothesis. But with his Iranian accent it came out "Don be thoopid." He went on, "She's in jail."

It turns out that Gretchen's daughter had sticky fingers. Farhad knew the whole story, told by Gretchen herself after eliciting a promise that he wouldn't tell anybody. Farhad apparently felt I met this criterion.

"Oh yeth," he went on. "Gretchen said the problem started when the daughter was only five years old and stole a candy bar from a convenience store. By junior high she was stealing clothing from a department store, and then fifty thousand dollars from her employer."

He then added, just in case I might not have been able to figure it out myself, "But it wasn't the candy bar that sent her to jail."

He provided other juicy details, most of which I've forgotten, before ending his monologue with the words, "Yes, poor Kleptomania. She broke her mother's heart."

"Wha-- *Kleptomania?*" I said. "That's not her name. You're making that up."

"Oh yes it is," he said solemnly. "It's on her birth certificate." Then he laughed like a fat baby, probably hoping I would ask Gretchen about her daughter "Kleptomania."

I didn't.

For eight Saturdays, Farhad and I sat next to each other at Early American reproduction desks situated two feet apart in the leasing office. The complex was, by Houston standards, upscale. I had moved in a year earlier, leasing a nice three-bedroom affair so my kids would have their own rooms when they visited. I don't know where Farhad lived.

In addition to our desks, the office consisted of two large wing-back chairs positioned on either side of a roaring fireplace -- an interesting architectural choice considering the temperature in Houston rarely dips much below 90 degrees. The fireplace, Gretchen explained, was "part of the ambiance."

When I complained to Farhad about having a fireplace

blazing away in 100+ degree heat, he said, "Yes, but at least we can roast our weenies."

I gave him a look -- I wasn't even sure he was really Iranian, much less gay or straight -- so I couldn't be sure if he was coming on to me, or just being a smartass. Maybe he had a package of hot dogs in the office refrigerator and thought we could roast them for lunch. I never asked.

The office also featured a formal dining room table centered under an enormous brass chandelier. It consisted of two dozen or so scrolled brass arms with candlesticks on the end, each with a little fabric lampshade. This table is where we seated people when it was time to sign the lease papers.

Tailored silk moire draperies were tied to the sides of French windows leading to a formally landscaped courtyard.

The place was called, believe it or not, "The Plantation." Not a real plantation, with cotton fields and mint juleps on the wraparound porch, but a large apartment complex built to look like a plantation, complete with huge white pillars lining the facade. It looked like a movie set for *Gone With the Wind.*

Within minutes of storming out, Mrs. Parker returned, but neither Farhad nor I lifted as much as an eyebrow, because she repeated this scene at least a half dozen times a day. For some reason I found it charming: she's British, and I'm a pushover for a British accent. She was also a dead ringer for Dame Maggie Smith.

Our "Dame" -- Penelope -- was extremely polite, but somewhat aloof. Her appearance was consistent with her manner. She was always perfectly coiffured and "coutured," and I don't recall ever seeing her in anything other than a St. John knit with a little leather handbag and sensible black leather pumps. People were more likely to confuse her with Queen Elizabeth than Lady Gaga.

Penelope Parker was also likable, and I liked her. True, she could seem imperious, frequently saying things like "I should be ever so grateful if someone would look in on my stove. It's taking the water for my tea a frightfully long time to boil."

God help the poor schlub who didn't jump when she said jump. In that sense she may have looked upon Farhad and me as her own personal Corgis, expecting us to beg and roll over -- and not pee on the carpet.

Still, I looked forward to her hourly visits. "Hello, Mrs. Parker," I'd say when she swept into the office. Or, just to show her what a bon vivant I could be, I'd sometimes say, "Bonjour, Madame. Comment ça va?" She loved that, and always replied with a long string of French, which became somewhat problematic since I do not speak or understand the language.

"Won't you have a seat?" I'd ask, switching to English. "And shall I get you some tea?"

As I offered tea, my instinct was to move toward the sterling silver tea service on the sideboard, but I soon learned not to do this. When I first started helping out in the office, Farhad showed me that the teapot was glued shut. Ditto the sugar bowl and creamer. They were glued firmly to the silver tray on which they sat, which in turn was glued to the sideboard. For all I knew, the sideboard itself was nailed to the floor. To pour a cup of tea, one would need to hoist the entire piece of furniture in the air and turn it upside down. "People steal anything," Farhad explained. And then, nodding toward Gretchen's empty office, he added, "Just ask her." I wondered if he was suggesting Gretchen was also glued into place, but then I realized he was referring to her sticky-fingered daughter.

Once, as a prank, after making Mrs. Parker's tea in the office microwave, as I usually did, I called out, "Mrs. Parker, would you mind getting a sugar cube or two from the tea service?" This should have made her suspicious, as we never asked her to do anything. She did the asking; we did the doing.

"Yes, of course," was her crisp reply, at which time I leaned around the door of the kitchen to watch as she approached the silver service. I suppressed my initial laugh when she struggled with the lid on the sugar bowl, and then tried to pick up the bowl itself -- to no avail. But I couldn't contain myself when she bent over to examine why nothing on the tray seemed to move. "Bloody hell!" I heard her whisper to herself as she pushed and pulled at it. I finally rushed to her side.

"No, no, Mrs. Parker. Don't bother. It's a little joke. You can't really use it; it's just for decoration. It's all glued to the sideboard. See?" I said, trying to budge the tray. She was not amused. She looked at me like I was an escaped mental patient before turning sharply and returning to the one wing-back chair which she had long ago designated as "hers."

"That's the silliest thing I ever heard of," was all she said about my prank. But I laughed about it all day long and she smiled slightly, which made it seem even funnier to me.

Mrs. Parker didn't wear well with many people, and Farhad in particular didn't seem to like her. He had a point: her demands were frequent and sometimes tiresome.

"Would it be too much trouble...," she would start. Or, "I do hate to be a bother, but...," followed by her latest complaint. Our maintenance crew liked her though: whenever we sent them down the hall to do something for her – which was often – they would receive a five or ten dollar tip as they left.

She gave the office personnel tips, too, but they weren't monetary. Her tips took the form of advice, such as the time she snapped at me, "Don't wear that tie again. It doesn't suit you." Or, to Farhad, "You need to learn to speak properly. Nobody understands a word you say."

It didn't take me long to see what was going on. She was lonely. She'd been a widow for at least ten years by the time I met her, but somehow I don't think she'd ever been able to "buck up," as the British say.

She didn't have a friend in the world -- nobody ever came to see her -- and I honestly don't remember when it was that I decided to take her under my wing, but we soon became friends out of the office. She didn't have a car, so she frequently asked me to take her here and there -- to the grocery store or post office, maybe, or occasionally to a chic little dress shop. She always offered to pay me for these little excursions, which I politely refused, but occasionally she would insist on buying me lunch, which was enjoyable for both of us.

From time to time she would call and demand that I come to her apartment for a gin and tonic, which I also liked. When the phone rang, she would say without preamble, "I've made a pitcher of G&T's. Come at once." I'd practically run to her apartment where I would find the door standing wide open. She greeted me with a drink served on a small linen cocktail napkin.

After several of these cocktail hours, I began giving her an air kiss and a slight embrace when we met outside the office -- she was by now my friend, after all, and I could see that she liked that.

We would sit for an hour or so as she talked and I would listen -- she was worse than Farhad once you wound her up -- but she was forgiven because her stories (unlike his) were fascinating. She had grown up in a village not far from London in an old manor house that had been in the family for generations. It had been chockablock full of art and antiques, but the collection had been severely whittled down to the four rooms she now occupied at The Plantation. But, oh, what beautiful things she had!

She shocked me one day, as we sat sipping, when she said, "I'm leaving all this to you, you know."

"What?" I said, incredulously. "Seriously?" I stammered. I hardly knew what to say. Finally I managed, "Well, that's a nice thought. Thank you for thinking of me that highly, but let's just hope you have many more years to enjoy them yourself."

She walked across the room and lifted a small, expensive-looking painting from its hook on the wall. "Here," she said, thrusting it at me. "Take this now."

"I certainly will not," I said. "I'm not taking any of your things. Here, let me put that back where it belongs." And I did.

I knew how she loved her things. They were, in a sense, her only friends, so I wasn't about to deny her the satisfaction they gave her. The realization of her situation made me sad. Other than me, and occasionally Farhad, there was nobody in Mrs. Parker's life.

When she proffered various objets d'art in the months to come, my answer was always the same: "Thank you, but no."

"Well, it will all be yours someday," she'd say, but even that made me uncomfortable. I tried to dissuade her, suggesting she leave everything to the Houston Art Museum or the library. "No," she said. "I shall leave it all to you."

I eventually moved into my own home and decided I had met my obligation to Gretchen, so my Saturdays at the Plantation came to an end. I am sorry to say that Penelope and I eventually lost touch. But after she died, I received a neatly rolled package from Farhad, accompanied by a note advising me that Mrs. Parker had left me a small Persian rug.

The remainder of her estate apparently went to him.

Drop Trou

Ever since Brad and I moved into our new home, we have been searching for a suitable piece of art for the dining room and, since the particular wall we are trying to fill is somewhat large, we are leaning toward an abstract piece. Modern art, we've found, seems to be bigger -- and not as expensive -- as the old masters.

After looking at every art gallery in town, I finally settled on a big blank canvas from an arts and crafts store onto which I glued a photo of a polar bear. Since the canvas is white and polar bears are white, I jokingly refer to it as "Polar Bear in a Snow Storm."

One of our guests asked if he could buy it.

In our household, interior decorating is usually left to me, and I take it seriously. By "seriously" I mean I Google a bunch of websites until I find what I'm looking for.

For example, on one site I found myself looking at a photograph labeled "Aurillac, France." Brad and I both like France, so the idea of an artistic photograph taken there had a certain appeal.

At first glance, the scene appeared to be a lovely field of oversized mushrooms. I know that doesn't sound very appealing, but they were evenly spaced over the rolling hillside and something about the symmetry and coloring of the piece made it quite attractive.

On closer examination, however, I discovered I wasn't looking at mushrooms but, rather, umbrellas. This seemed strange at first, but actually made perfect sense when I learned that Aurillac is the umbrella capital of France. According to Wikipedia, more than a quarter of a million umbrellas were made there in 1999, which generated around 100 jobs. If my math serves me correctly, this means each worker had to create at least ten umbrellas each day. For someone who has trouble just opening one umbrella without incident, this seems noteworthy.

What is most intriguing about this photo, however, is not so much the umbrellas but the fact that they are all being held high by naked people: *hundreds* of stark naked people, each holding an umbrella over his or her head.

When I told Brad about this, he said, "Are you sure they're alive?"

"Alive?" I sputtered. "Of course they're alive! Whoever heard of dead people holding umbrellas?"

"No, I mean, are you sure they aren't mannequins?"

I had to show him the on-line photo so he could see, without a doubt, that indeed they were alive. One gentleman in particular proved without a doubt that they were alive.

The artist/photographer of this piece is a man by the name of Spencer Tunick, a New Yorker who specializes in photographing large groups of naked people in various settings. That's quite a speciality. Back in the days when there were telephone directories, I suppose his category heading would have been "Photographers -- Naked People" just above "Photographers -- Wedding."

And by "large groups," I don't mean a few dozen people standing around saying "cheese." To date, Mr. Tunick has created more than 75 "human installations" in various places, including more than 18,000 people who agreed to be photographed sans clothing -- *sin ropa* -- in Mexico City's famed Zocalo Square. That's eighteen *thousand* people.

That sounded interesting and artistic, so I searched for that piece online, but not necessarily for our dining room wall. People are finicky, and I couldn't imagine that many of our dinner guests would enjoy gazing at 18,000 backsides as they enjoyed their rump roast.

Still, the photo had a certain appeal. Just as the Aurillac umbrellas first looked like mushrooms, the naked Mexicans looked like a caramel-colored shag rug. There were so many of them that they leaked out into the street leading to the square.

I studied that photograph closely and, truth be told, all the others in Mr. Tunick's extensive portfolio. In one photo, I saw hundreds of naked people lying face down on top of large wine barrels in Burgundy. In another, the bodies on Surfer's Beach at Montauk look like beached pink seals -- some of them perilously close to washing back out to sea. At Gaasbeek Castle in Belgium, several dozen naked men held their swords aloft as if preparing to sacrifice some poor guy lying posed on a tree trunk. That one was especially creepy, and since the motif of our dining room doesn't include sacrificial offerings I decided it might not be a good choice, either.

One of my favorites was taken in Herefordshire, England, where all the naked people were either a lovely shade of lavender or taxi-cab yellow. From a distance, it looked like a field of flowers. But close up you can easily tell these are really naked human beings. I can't imagine the time it would take to body paint that many people, so I assume the color was Photoshopped.

As I examined the various photos, I couldn't help but wonder what it would be like to get naked with that many people.

A disturbing series of three photos taken in Ohio drove home the point. The first featured several thousand naked people lying face-down on a bridge. Nothing too exciting there, especially since I had just seen 18,000 people buck naked in Mexico City.

The second photo showed a few thousand naked people lying on their sides in front of a ship in the background. If you squint your eyes, it actually looks like the ship is moving through pink waves.

But it was the third photo that brought back a memory I had long suppressed. The photo was of men only -- thousands of them -- hunched over, butts in the air, in front of -- what else -- a football stadium.

It bothered me, I realized, not because I worry about our culture's obsession with football, but because it reminded me of the last time I had to bend over naked in a room full of men.

It was 1969, and the war in Vietnam was in full force. I was 21 and had been safely ensconced in college for a couple of years when, as a result of my haphazard study habits and propensity to party, I flunked French. The rest of my grades weren't all that great either, so I was placed on "academic suspension" -- a euphemism for "get your act together and stop wasting our time." I suddenly discovered I was free to skip classes as much as I liked, since I didn't have any. I was no longer considered a student of the University of Colorado. *Persona non grata.* My banishment was scheduled to last one year. I prayed I wouldn't get drafted.

But the Selective Service System was obviously not on my prayer chain. They seemed to get word of my suspension almost as quickly as I did, and my 2-S deferment quickly became 1-A: "available for unrestricted military service."

Even though I knew it was coming, when the notice arrived I couldn't have been less prepared. I love my country and consider myself a proud American, but I was also confused about the war. College campuses everywhere were filled with anti-war demonstrations, and while I never attended one I, too, was angry with my government. At the same time, I had great respect for the troops -- I just didn't want to be one of them.

But Uncle Sam didn't care what I wanted so I was ordered to report for processing at the U.S. Customs Building in downtown Denver.

I was to appear at 9 o'clock one morning. I parked in a lot across the street and sat in my car, hoping to put off the inevitable as long as possible. Soon, something in the next car caught my eye, and I turned to see that it was occupied by a guy who looked about my age. He was staring off into space. Looking around, I could see there were other men in nearby cars, sitting and staring at nothing in particular. I wasn't alone. As nine o'clock approached, car doors began to open, as if on cue, discharging drivers who walked, zombie-like, across the street and into the Customs Building. Nobody said a word.

Inside the big double doors leading to the Selective Service office, arrows on the wall and floor directed us. After completing numerous forms we were told to strip to our underwear, which caused some kid to quip, "Just like strip poker?" We laughed, but it was nervous laughter for sure.

Then we were called, one at a time, into a series of small, inner offices.

The first contained a doctor who stuck an instrument into each of my ears. He then wrote something down and directed me to the next door. It was all very private, which is good, because I don't want just anybody staring into my ears.

In the next room, also private, I was given a standard eye exam: "Cover one eye and use your finger to point which direction the letters on the chart are leaning." I noticed that the doctor wasn't paying any attention to which way I pointed, so I completed the entire test with my eyes closed. In a voice which barely concealed his boredom he intoned, "Third line...," and I pointed at the ceiling, then the door, then down my pants. He never looked up. He wrote something on the form -- probably "Smartass" -- and I was sent to the next room.

This continued as I moved from one small room to the next, seeing only the one professional who was administering that particular portion of my physical. It was all very assembly line.

At one point my hearing was checked by a middle-aged

man who had one of those faces that doesn't show any emotion whatsoever. Either that, or he had just come from the dentist and his entire face was numb. He didn't say a single word. He could have been animatronic, for all I know. When I entered his little room, he gestured for me to sit at a machine and then handed me a set of earphones. He slowly turned the various dials on his equipment until I heard a piercing sound in one ear or the other which caused my eyes to fly open wide. This was apparently proof enough that I could hear that particular tone, at which point the ear phones went dead and a new sound gradually appeared. I shudder to think about what might have happened if I'd failed to look at him when I heard each sound -- maybe he would have just kept dialing the volume up until my head blew off. This went on for a few minutes until he stood up and gestured for me to take off the earphones. I did, and he jerked his head toward the next door, which was obviously a directive to move on. As I left I smiled at the irony of having my hearing checked by someone who appeared to be mute. Who needs to hear when nobody's talking?

Next was the tickle-your-feet room, where the doctor carefully examined me for fungus, flat-footedness and several other maladies that he talked about but which I no longer remember. The two things I do remember about him was that he really did tickle each of my feet, forcing me to squirm and laugh when what I really wanted to do was smack him. I would swear that he also counted my toes, moving his lips as he did. It seems to me that someone who looks at feet all day could spot a missing or an extra toe without having to actually count them.

Next I was sent into a room where the doctor ran a cold

stethoscope all over my chest. My nipples got hard, which I took to mean I passed the test.

I didn't like the next room where the doctor began pounding on my knee with a hammer. This provoked the reactive kick he seemed to be looking for, but it hurt, so I kicked him a second time without being asked.

By this time I began to feel uneasy. There wasn't much left to do, and I had a hunch the next little exam room would contain a doctor who might want to see my junk.

But the next room wasn't little at all. It was as big as a gymnasium and, by the time I arrived, it was chock full of other guys who were standing around in their underwear. I didn't like the looks of it, so I began to put my clothes back on.

"What are you doing, man?" a guy next to me asked.

"I'm getting dressed, obviously. What else?"

He looked at me like I was crazy, but before he could say anything, a big guy in Army fatigues screamed "Atten-shun!" and we all stood up straight as if we already knew the drill.

"Line up, gentlemen!" he screamed. His voice was angry and mean, like he was getting ready to beat us up. It scared me so much I almost grabbed the hand of the guy next to me and asked if we could be buddies. Fortunately for me, he had already moved to the line painted around the perimeter of the room, so I went over and toed the line, too.

The sergeant resumed barking.

"Now. Gentlemen." Each word was clipped as though it formed its own sentence. "Here. Is. What. I. Want. You. To. Do."

He told us to leave a distance between ourselves and the

man next to us. "Exactly. Twelve. Inches. Apart." I didn't have a ruler and would gladly have offered to run home and get one, but I seemed to be the only person without the God-given ability to measure exactly twelve inches with my naked eye, so I simply spaced myself evenly between the guys on my right and left.

Naturally, I looked around to see what kind of underwear everybody was wearing. Why not? I quickly determined that we were about half and half: half briefs and half boxers. Boxers have a certain mystery about them -- they aren't any more revealing than a swim suit or pair of baggy shorts, so nobody knows for sure what treasure lies within. Briefs, on the other hand, leave little to the imagination.

I was wearing briefs, of course.

It took about five seconds for everybody in the room to notice the one guy who might have had a particular deferment in mind. He was wearing pink women's panties.

Pink! I was about to whisper to the guy next to me, but once again the drill sergeant was screaming at us.

"Ten-shun!"

I froze, as I would in the children's yard game, "Statue." I had one hand poised to tap my neighbor on the shoulder and the other covering my mouth since I was about to whisper. I looked ridiculous, since all the others guys stood ramrod straight, backs straight, chins jutted forward, arms notably at the side.

I barely had time to pull myself together before he screamed, "Drop. Trou!"

Well, we don't call our underwear "trou" in my family, so I was tempted to just stand there until he made it clear what he really wanted us to do. I doubt he would have been amused, and I certainly would have been alone, since every other man in that room -- at least a hundred of us -- dropped his underwear to the floor with the precision of the Rockettes. Since probably 99 percent of these guys were heterosexual, all eyes remained straight ahead, focused on the far wall or the ceiling.

Only one person appeared to be looking around. Me.

My viewing pleasure was quickly interrupted when Sarge screamed "About. Face!" Now we were looking at the wall, so I had no choice but to keep my eyes on what appeared to be a remnant of Scotch tape stuck to the paint.

The next thing we heard was, "Legs. Apart. And. Bend. Over!" At least now I had a view again -- although looking upside down and backwards through my own legs wasn't exactly the perspective I was looking for.

In time, several doctors began rolling around the perimeter of the room on little squeaky-wheeled stools, each accompanied by an assistant holding a tray. A rubber glove was donned, a digit inserted into a waiting butt, and the glove discarded. Roll to next man. There were a couple of sniggers and more than a few exclamations of "Hey!" -- maybe they were expecting to hike a football and were therefore surprised and disappointed.

A few minutes later I stood in front of the Sergeant himself who, examining the paperwork my family physician had provided, asked if it was true that I had asthma. "Yes," I admitted, not quite sure why that would interest him. "Deferred!" he barked as he stamped my paperwork.

This little trip down memory lane made me realize that while Mr. Tunick's naked crowd photos may not find a place on our dining room wall, at least now I know that I am well-qualified to be a participant in one of his photo shoots -- especially if it takes place at the local Selective Service office.

Tiny Town

In the hills west of Denver, a long time ago in a galaxy far away...

Oh. Sorry. That's *Star Wars*. Let's begin again.

In the hills west of Denver there exists a land where all the inhabitants must be less than thirty inches tall. This eliminates adults, except maybe Danny Devito or Peter Dinklage, and most big dogs. Most kindergartners qualify, although anyone who has ever lived with a kindergartner will tell you that an entire town full of them would be torn to pieces in no time.

I'd love to say this is where I grew up, but it wasn't. I was permitted to visit only once a year or, if I could convince my grandmother that the visit we took only a month earlier had actually taken place a year ago, twice.

This lilliputian place was called, appropriately, Tiny Town, and it still operates today -- some 90 years after it first flung open its little doors.

I was probably two or three years old the first time I was taken to Tiny Town -- and that's how old my kids were the first time my wife and I took them.

I don't remember the specifics of my first visit, but I do remember peeing in my pants because I was having too much fun to take a break. Ironically, this is a problem I still have -- not peeing in my pants, but feeling too busy to stop whatever I'm doing to go to the bathroom.

Tiny Town is every kid's dream. The adults tower over all the buildings like Gulliver or King Kong, while kids roam in and out of the little houses like the miniature people they are. When she was quite young, my daughter went inside one of the nicer houses in town (it was the biggest and most opulent, naturally) and refused to come out. "I like it in here," she said through the little window. "I'm going to live here."

I had to give that some serious thought since she had been pretty whiny all day, and maybe a few weeks on her own would do her good. My wife disagreed and offered her little treats if she would come out, the way a person would wiggle a dog biscuit in front of a dog. I told her she could stay in her little house but that she would have to get a little job so she could make her little house payments and buy her little groceries.

I thought that was pretty funny, so I had a little smile on my face. My wife didn't, and she shot me a dirty little look.

There are over a hundred buildings in Tiny Town and I've been in -- or looked in -- every single one of them dozens of times. The place fascinates young and old alike, probably because it makes us feel omnipotent. When it is possible to see all the activities of an entire town from a single vantage point, you wonder if that's what it's like to be God.

No trip to Tiny Town was complete without a ride (or

two, depending on how much one was willing to whine) on the Tiny Town Railroad -- an impressive collection of four fully-operating steam locomotives, each of which pulls six cars of screaming kids around a half-mile track.

This is one of those times when parents get the last laugh. Kids who throw a tantrum until they are allowed to ride the miniature train soon shut up when a hot ash from the steam boiler sets their hair on fire. Parents are seen grinning from ear to ear as their brats fly by with a look of terror on their dirty little faces.

I'm not exaggerating the look of terror. A few years ago, five of the six cars on the Tiny Town Train tipped over when it went screeching around the corner at, according to a newspaper story, "12-17 miles per hour." People were injured, but nobody was killed as far as I know -- which is just as well, since I doubt there is a little mortuary among the collection of Tiny Town buildings.

But I'm sure it was a big little mess.

My own childhood visits to Tiny Town were often accompanied by two of my cousins, Donna and Linda. Our grandmother would pick us up -- I was always the first to be picked up and the last to be dropped off because she liked me best -- and I mention that only because I plan to give them each a copy of this book -- and we would all drive up to the mountains. That trip would take less than twenty minutes these days, but back then it seemed like hours in a hot, un-air-conditioned car. In order to keep us from filling up on "junk," as Grandmother called it, she would bring along a picnic lunch.

On one memorable occasion we managed to find the only spot in blazing sunshine, while less than twenty feet away beckoned a canopy of shade from the forest surrounding us.

"Oh, it's so nice and warm here," Grandmother said, spreading a blanket on the ground. "Let's just sit in the sun."

I had to admit, the sun felt good, and I could amuse myself by watching my skin create permanent freckles right before my eyes which my little friends would eventually take to calling "fairy kisses" -- but I'm not bitter.

As I was thus occupied, Grandmother waited for the mayonnaise on the sandwiches to warm up. Donna and Linda, meanwhile, wandered off looking for dirt and happened to make a startling discovery at the other side of the blanket: a line of red ants -- the kind that sting -- marching toward us like the Charge of the Light Brigade. Grandmother was busy, so the girls and I simply watched as a hundred or so -- quickly growing to a thousand and then a hundred million -- red ants took up residence on our blanket.

I wanted to use Linda's glasses as a magnifier to see how they liked the heat close-up, but she wouldn't let me.

The ants continued to make a bee-line (the bees were bringing up the rear) toward the food, but suddenly veered off, into my underpants. I began screaming, "Ants in my pants! Ants in my pants!" and dancing around like I meant it. Upon later examination we saw that the little buggers had zeroed in on each of my newly formed freckles, making them 3-D, like measles.

Grandmother, not realizing these were real ants and that I was being bitten to death, found my dance greatly amusing, as though I had invented it on the spot for her viewing pleasure. But when the girls started screaming too, and she saw that the pattern on the blanket seemed to be alive, she jumped up and started dancing too. There we were, three kids and an old lady, jumping around in the forest clearing like Indians doing a rain dance.

Grandmother eventually grabbed the blanket from the ground and began to shake it vigorously -- ants flying everywhere, but mostly into my hair. For years when any of us wanted something from Grandmother all we had to say was, "Do you remember that time you made us sit on top of an anthill, Grandmother?" We usually got what we wanted after that.

Pool! Pool!

Brad and I once spent a wonderful week in Cancun, Mexico. We stayed in a suite at a fancy resort which featured, among other things, two of the biggest swimming pools I have ever seen. Each pool had a swim-up bar in which you could sit on underwater concrete stools while slurping your slurpee. People who drink too much fall off their stool and drown. In addition, round-the-clock food and beverage service was available, which involved waiters stopping by every two or three minutes to ask if they can bring you anything.

I felt it only polite to reply, "Yes, of course."

We were invited as the guests of our friends and next door neighbors Helen and Geoff, who paid all the resort expenses, including restaurant meals, drinks from morning 'til night, and even additional meals which Helen prepared and served in our *en suite* dining room.

So now I suppose I have to write them a thank-you note.

As the four of us sat by the pool one afternoon, I kept busy trying to determine the relative advantages of a

Margarita versus a Mai-Tai. As my eyes were rolling around in my head, I happened to notice a human being flying through the air, which, in my drunken haze, looked like a very big insect. He was waving his arms frantically as if he were about to crash land.

I sent him a friendly wave. "Hola!" I cried.

It turns out he wasn't about to die after all. He was merely doing what is popularly known as "parasailing," which is a sporty-sounding name for flying through the air while dangling from a thin canopy of fabric which is attached to the back of a speedboat by a long piece of string.

I know this for a fact, because I did it once myself.

It was some thirty years or so ago, when I was still married, but the memory is as fresh today as the headache I've had since the completion of my Margarita experiment...

My wife and I had decided to take a quick trip to Acapulco to escape the winter snow. I can't remember if our children were born yet, but if they were, we must have left them in the airport parking lot, because they weren't with us when we got on the plane.

We arrived late for our flight, which wasn't that unusual back then, and it wasn't a big deal -- you simply hustled out to the gate and jumped on the plane. Airport security, as we know it today, hadn't been invented yet, so parking your car was as simple as pulling into a space a few hundred feet from the front door. I know of people who were running so late they simply drove up to the door, jumped out, and threw their keys to a Sky Cap and said, "Take care of this for me, will you? I'll be back in a week!"

Try doing that these days. While you're trying to figure out what a "Sky Cap" is, your car will be blown up by the bomb squad.

Our hometown airline in those days was Continental, which was known for its superb service and therefore no longer exists. I loved flying Continental, whose slogan once was "We really move our tail for you." And they really did. Flight attendants greeted you warmly, offered you a pre-departure beverage and, when it was time to eat, lowered the tray table for you and covered it with a starched white placemat. The food tray came with miniature glass salt and pepper shakers, and your silverware was a reasonable facsimile of sterling silver. Your water glass was, well, glass. And that was in coach class! I can't imagine what it was like in first class -- steak flambé served table-side, I assume.

I had mixed feelings about the little printed prayer card that was discreetly placed under the silverware -- I wondered if company management knew something we didn't know, something that might require an in-flight prayer.

On this particular flight we enjoyed a nice lunch, and my wife settled back for a nap (the seats actually leaned back -- and I don't mean into the lap of the guy behind you) while I browsed through the current issue of a magazine the flight attendant allowed me to choose from her little cart.

The magazine I chose had a story about the Mexican resort we were headed to, so I read it carefully. It contained some lovely photographs, and one of them caught my eye: a handsome young man dangling in the sky from a parachute. Earlier I'd told my wife that our resort offered "transit from airplane to resort," and I briefly wondered if this was what they had in mind: the plane would come in low and drop us by parachute directly into the hotel.

As I studied the photo more carefully, I could see that both the boat and the parachutist appeared to be heading out to sea -- blithely unaware that their next stop would probably be South America. Still, he looked like he was having a good time, so it wasn't hard to imagine myself in the same circumstances: a human kite sailing through the air.

Except for one thing. I'm not big on heights. I get sweaty palms at higher elevations -- which is somewhat of a problem since, for most of my life, I've lived more than a mile above sea level (but since I can't see the sea, I am blissfully unaware.) I haven't sought professional help for my condition, but apparently it is a real -- and not uncommon -- affliction. It should be noted that parasailing is not usually prescribed as a treatment.

When my wife awakened from her nap, I showed her the magazine article and, pointing to the photo of the guy flying through the air, I said, "I'm going to do that."

"Yeah, right," she said. She knew I had trouble standing on a kitchen step-stool.

It wasn't an idle boast, but I didn't intend to make good on it within the hour.

As soon as we checked in at the resort, we changed into swim wear and headed to the beach. We couldn't have walked ten yards onto the sand before a Mexican kid came running up to me saying, "Señor, Señor! You want to do dee parachute?"

I looked at my wife, wondering how she had managed

to alert them of my plan.

"Si," I said, using all of my Spanish. "I want to do it, but not quite yet..."

He nodded his head vigorously, as though he understood perfectly -- which he clearly did not. "Si, Si! Come dees way. Come dees way...," he said, pulling me by the arm.

"Not yet, not yet!" I said. I realized I was saying everything twice, as he had done. Was this how people who didn't speak Spanish were able to communicate with the locals?

He nodded vigorously. "Si, Si!" -- and he continued to pull me toward the water. My wife tagged along like Prissy tagged along after Scarlet in *Gone With the Wind*. Clearly, she didn't think this was going to happen, but she didn't want to miss it if it did.

When we reached the water, I saw a large expanse of silk -- a parachute -- stretched out from the edge of the water onto the sand. A leather harness was attached to a rope which terminated at the back of a speedboat bobbing in the water in front of us.

I began to have second thoughts.

"Dees way, Señor! Dees way!" the kid said, picking up the harness and holding it like a red cape in the bullring.

"Not yet," I said slowly, as if to a slow child. "Not yet." Seeing the confusion on his face, I added, "I just want to think about it for a few minutes...maybe watch somebody else do it first...."

He smiled and nodded -- and began strapping me into the harness. At this point an older kid came up and said sharply, as if trying to rouse someone from a coma, "Señor! It is fifty pesos. You can pay when you get back." Then, in what was apparently Mexican black humor, he added, "If you don't come back, you don't have to pay!"

My wife, who had been silent up to this point, laughed maniacally at this joke. I scowled at her.

The older kid continued, picking up a rope with a blue rag tied to it. "Señor!" he shouted again. "When I yell, 'Pull!' you pull on this rope," he said, placing the rope in my hand. "When I say, 'Don't pull,' you let go. *Comprende?*"

"Si," I said, grateful to have another opportunity to show off my Spanish. And then, for added emphasis, I said again, "Si."

Then, without forewarning, he turned to a man in the boat and screamed, "Go!"

And with that, the big kid and little kid each grabbed one of my legs and, carrying me, wishbone style, ran toward the water -- even as the speedboat was racing away from us into the ocean. When we got to the edge, they lifted me into the air and gracefully threw me...into the water.

Now the boat was pulling me out to sea -- head first, face down, and mouth open. I don't know how much sea water I consumed before the parachute began to fill with air and slowly sucked me out of the water and up, up, up into the air.

Unfortunately, the harness was beginning to fall off -- but this wasn't apparent until I was at least two million feet up in the sky. At the same time I realized my lungs were full of water and I was drowning, even as I soared peacefully toward South America.

I tried to remember my junior lifesaving course and

realized I would have to perform artificial resuscitation on myself -- since there wasn't anybody else to do it.   I quickly folded my arms over my chest -- which had the added advantage of tightening the harness -- and began compressions.   Somehow it worked and I began spitting up Pacific Ocean water. Gallons of it.

Eventually, it became very quiet -- which meant I was either dead or awfully high up in the air. Deciding I was still alive, I looked down -- only to discover that the people on the beach had been replaced by ants. The big hotels that lined the beach upon our arrival were now little Monopoly hotels along a boardwalk.

It was beautiful.

I could also see the speedboat weaving through the waves as the pilot made his way down the coast and then, after executing a wide turn, back again.

My ears were still full of water and probably fish guts, but I began to hear a small, high-pitched whisper that sounded like, "Pool...pool!"

Pool? What pool? I looked at the swimming pools in front of each hotel. Ah, yes...pools...yes...lots of them...

The little voice got bigger. "Pool! Pool!" it said.

Pool? Oh! *Pull!* I finally realized one of the little ants was screaming "pull" at me. Once I got it, I grabbed the rope with the blue rag and pulled.

Nothing.

The force of the air filling the parachute made the rope taut. It wouldn't budge. Letting go of the harness, I put both hands on the rope and pulled with all my might. This created a gap in the canopy of the parachute and I began dropping -- plummeting, really -- toward the earth at top speed.

I heard that little voice again. "Doan pool! Doan pool!"

Wha...? Oh. *Don't pull.*

I let go, and the slit closed up and the parachute started flying again -- this time toward a seven-story hotel on the beach. As best I could determine, I would meet the hotel on the fifth floor, carving a Rex-shaped hole in the side.

"Pool! Pool!" This time I moved quickly, since I was on a collision course with a very hard-looking building. Now I could see that the ants on the beach were really people and they were all watching me with their mouths hanging open, as in shock.

"Doan pool!" This time there wasn't time for a repeat of the instruction because the two kids who had initially thrown me into the ocean were now running toward me, arms outstretched to catch me, which they did -- but not without an audible grunt, as if they were catching a bag of cement.

But I was back on *terra firma* and would have kissed it in thanks, except I'd already swallowed too much sand for one day.

My wife came walking up like she'd just come from a manicure, but I noticed that she had our Super8 movie camera in her hand.

"Did you see that?" I said, excitedly. "I almost died!"

"Yes, I did," she said cooly. "I got the whole thing on film."

I was impressed, and told her so. "Wow. I can't believe you had the presence of mind to capture the whole thing as it was happening. How did you think to do that?"

"Easy," she said. "I wanted it for insurance purposes."

Notes From The Jungle

I am in the jungle as I write this.

Well, not the jungle actually, but close to some trees, which is almost the same thing. Everywhere I look I can see pine trees and mountain tops. Beneath my feet are pine needles and dirt. This is as rustic as it gets for me, even though, if I look over my shoulder I can see a shopping center.

This place is called Bergen Park, Colorado, and while it is only thirty minutes from downtown Denver, for me it may as well be the outback.

I am seated at a primitive picnic table, with hundreds of initials carved into the top. The base of the table consists of a concrete framework, just as Native Americans or early settlers might have used.

I didn't notice it when I chose this particular spot, but now I see that there is a bathroom facility -- an "outhouse" -- within twenty yards of my table. Over the next hour I will be able to keep my eyes on the feet of various men and women who enter the facility and, in fact, where they go once they are inside -- since the walls do not reach the ground. I would never be able to go in there, since I can see how easy it would be for the local fauna to slip under the walls and bite the occupant on the you-know-what.

There are people, I realize, who enjoy being outdoors and will shun any semblance of the modern world -- even tents, sleeping bags, gas stoves, etc. -- but I am not one of these people. The closest I've ever come to even considering a true outdoor adventure was when Brad told me that in Nepal, where he has hiked, porters carry such things as tents, stoves, and portable toilets. But on further reflection I realized he didn't say "hot running water," so I had to decline.

Today is a stark reminder that I am a modern kind of guy. Since I come from the twenty-first century, my laptop is sitting on this wooden table. Its lighted screen serves as a clarion call to all local insects who probably have never seen anything so silly, and have come by to take a look. They use my arms as their landing strips, and some of them try to create little outposts in my ears. I punctuate each sentence I type by slapping various body parts because I feel as though I am crawling with bugs. I'm sure the people who just walked out of the outhouse think something is seriously wrong with me.

But it isn't true that the "great outdoors" is entirely foreign to me. While growing up, I was forcibly enrolled in the Boy Scouts of America, after I completed a brief and boring period spent making bird houses and plaster of Paris paperweights in Cub Scouts.

Other than those bird houses and plaster paperweights, the only thing I remember about Cub Scouts is that my den mother, Mrs. Boehmer, had two-inch long fingernails worthy of the *Guiness Book of World Records*. Even more exciting, she had breasts as big as basketballs. If you were injured in any way during our weekly meeting, Mrs. Boehmer swept you into her arms and buried your head between her basketballs. You've never seen such a group of uncoordinated little boys: the Keystone Cops were more agile than we were. One of us was always getting hurt and, as a result, one of us always had his head buried in Mrs. Boehmer's ample bosom. There is no question in my mind that many of those boys earned a dozen merit badges motivated solely by their desire to nuzzle Mrs. Boehmer's bosom.

I hated the Boy Scouts. I will grudgingly admit that it was well-run and that some of my fellow scouts no doubt benefited from it enormously -- but mostly these were boys who would otherwise have ended up as Crips, Bloods or Neo-Nazis. For them, Boy Scouts was a life-saver. For me, it was life-threatening.

One of the primary activities in Scouting is outdoor camping. For most people this brings to mind idyllic scenes of tents, campfires, "s'mores" and boy-bonding. For me, it conjures up memories of frozen digits, death marches through the woods, food cooked with dirt as a seasoning, and torture.

Boy Scout camp was bad enough, but at least it was indoors -- or what passes for indoors in the woods. In the summer, camp comprised dozens of tents with wooden floors and folding cots on which your could unroll your sleeping bag so the snakes had to work harder to reach you. There was also a lake, in which you were expected to swim competitively out to the icebergs floating in the middle.

I attended Boy Scout summer camp only once, and I spent the entire time bawling my eyes out and complaining that I was homesick.   Since I hated everything about home, that proves just how bad it was at camp.

Winter outings were held at the same camp, which was now blanketed with three feet of snow. Since the road to the camp was closed during winter, we had to trudge through all that snow in order to reach the edge of the frozen lake. (We noted that the block of ice in the middle now extended all the way to the shore line.) The summer tents were stored for the winter, of course, and I can only assume they hid the wooden floor platforms so we wouldn't chop them up as firewood.

Which meant we had to carry in our own tents. I don't think nylon had been invented yet, so our tents were made of heavy canvas. Unless one of us had a mule, we had to lug our tents into the woods tied onto our backs like a dead body. Our sleeping bags were large cloth envelopes stuffed with what felt like sand and wet newspapers. Camping pots and pans weren't made of lightweight aluminum back then, as they are now but, rather, of cast iron -- the type used in the manufacture of ship anchors. Our feet were shod in boots which were heavy but not waterproof. My parents bought me socks that were so light you could see through them. As I recall, my gloves were blue from the tips of my fingers to my wrists. The only problem was, I didn't have gloves. Those were my actual hands, and they were blue.

My hat for these outings might well have been a beanie with a propeller for all the warmth it provided.   My stepmother gave me what she claimed was a warm coat --

but it was made of fur, which caused the other boys to refer to me as Jayne Mansfield. They wouldn't walk too close to me either, because one of the boys remarked that it was hunting season and from the back I looked like a grizzly bear.

The real terror began when the sun went down -- about three-thirty in the afternoon. The Scoutmaster ordered us to gather wood, but most of us just roamed around the vicinity whimpering, because any wood that might be on the ground would have required digging through several feet of snow. Some of the bigger boys did comply, however, because they were pyromaniacs-in-training and needed to practice their skills so they could later burn down their own homes.

Once the fire was roaring, we all circled around it. The other Scouts determined which side of the fire they would sit on based on where I sat -- because they knew from experience that the smoke would come to me. I dealt with this problem by sitting there with my eyes closed, until I became afraid that my eyelids were about to burn off. When I moved to the other side of the campfire, the smoke followed me so everybody else had to move, too.

In time, we thawed enough to retire to our tents where we would entertain each other by telling stories of people who froze to death during the night and whose bodies were torn to bits by roving bands of wolves.

A friend asked me much later if I knew I was gay when I was in the Boy Scouts. Well, yes, but I would have sooner cut my arm off with my Boy Scout knife than admit it. The culture of the Boy Scouts required members to be "trustworthy, loyal, helpful, friendly, courteous, kind, obedient, cheerful, thrifty, brave, clean, and reverent." And straight.

I never really wanted to be a Boy Scout but, oh, did I want to be straight.

Fifth Floor, Please

People talk about climbing the "ladder to the top," although I've noticed that for some, the ladder is more of an escalator that seems to be operated by brown-nosing the boss.

My own experience in the workplace was somewhat different.

When I was climbing the corporate ladder, I arduously stretched one hand above the other to grab each rung. I hoisted myself one step at a time, even as I saw some friends speed by on the brown-nose escalator. I didn't like them for passing me, but I desperately wanted to do the same thing.

I would eventually learn that since I wasn't permitted on that particular escalator, I would need to do the next best thing: I'd take the elevator.

I am, if anything, determined. When I decided that I needed to aspire to something other than busboy, hotel clerk or bank teller, I sat down with the want ads to decide what I wanted to be.

For those younger than age sixty, the "want ads" were

what we had before Craigslist. They were short printed job listings found in the Classified section of the newspaper. A "newspaper" was how people got the news before television, and television is how we got the news before the Internet. Oh, never mind.

Let's just say I went looking for a new job. During my search, I discovered that a local company had just been designated "The Best Place To Work in Denver." This company was reported to have the highest salaries and best benefits. Even better for me: they were hiring.

In other words, right up my career alley.

I assumed that all I would need to do was walk in and get to work.

I updated my resumé, bought a new suit, and made my way to the Employee Relations department. I did my homework, too. I knew they were in the oil business and that they had 2,500 employees.

They were about to get number 2,501.

The only problem was, I didn't know oil from ink. I didn't know how it came out of the ground, how it was refined, or even how it found its way from the refinery to the gas pump. Worse, I once had to ask somebody how to open the little trick door where the gas goes into the car.

I also didn't know anything about petroleum accounting, geology or engineering.

When the receptionist told me I would be interviewed by the director of the department -- the top guy -- I thought I'd won the lottery. I found out later that the reason for this was simple: they had hundreds of applicants each day, and they were understaffed, so this man was forced to work the front lines, just like everybody else.

He shook my hand, flipped his head toward a chair where I assumed he wanted me to sit, and sat silently as he read my resumé. This only took a few seconds, after which he stood and said, "Well, thank-you for coming by, but I can see from your resumé that you don't have any of the skills we are looking for right now."

"Wha...?" I had just settled in my chair and I certainly wasn't ready to go home. "But...," I stammered. "What skills are you looking for? Maybe I just forgot to put them on my resumé...."

"I doubt it," he said, his hand on the door knob. "Are you an engineer?"

"Well, no...."

"A geologist?"

"Well, no, but..."

"How about oil and gas accounting? Have you done that?"

"Well no, but I can certainly learn -- and I'm willing to start at the bottom and work my way up."

At this, he actually scoffed. "Yeah, well, I'm sorry but we don't have time to train you. Thanks for coming by."

And with that, he left the room.

I remained there for several minutes, frozen in disbelief. I looked around the office -- an interview room, I realized -- and briefly considered just staying there until they threw me out. "Oh. I must have misunderstood," I would say. "When you said you didn't have anything for me, I thought you said I was hired!"

I eventually found my way home but, after sleeping on it that night, I awakened with new determination. I decided I wasn't going to take no for an answer, and that the man who had interviewed me was just an idiot who had made a terrible mistake. I was sure that when he saw me again he would change his mind and hire me on the spot. So I put on the same suit, grabbed another copy of my resumé, and went back downtown.

It turned out he was a bit slow to realize he'd made a mistake. When the receptionist called to tell him I was waiting, I could sense there was silence at the other end of the line. Finally, I heard him say, "I'll be right out."

When he appeared he seemed slightly miffed.

"Hello, Mr. Williams," I said. "I don't know if you remember me...."

"Of course I remember you. You were here just yesterday."

"Exactly," I said, "And I was thinking last night...."

"And I told you we didn't have anything for you."

"Yes, that's right," I said. "You did. But I was thinking...."

"Well, that hasn't changed overnight," he said. "We still don't. And we won't tomorrow, or the next day. But we will call you if something comes up." And with that, he was gone.

In other words, "Don't call us, we'll call you."

Now I was angry. I hadn't had a chance to tell him that I would do anything -- and I had even practiced saying that so it didn't sound like I was coming on to him. I had already decided that I could be a file clerk, or elevator operator -- or anything, just to get my foot in the door. I made up my mind. I would go back again the next day.

I wish I could say that he relented, or that he opened his arms to welcome me into the company fold that third day...or even Monday of the following week, or Tuesday of the week after that.

He didn't. If anything, I could see new creases in his forehead -- anger lines, you might call them -- every time he came out to greet me, just as trees develop new rings with each growing season.

Finally, on my seventh visit, he seemed to be trying to decide whether he should call security or hire me just to shut me up. Fortunately, he decided to hire me.

"Come with me," he barked.

We returned to the same interview room where we'd started several weeks earlier. Before the door was closed, he whirled around and spoke directly into my nose. "Look. I don't think this will work and I just want you to know I will look for any reason to fire you, but I can tell you are one determined son-of-a-bitch, so I'll give you one chance to prove yourself. You can start tomorrow, right here in my department."

I could hardly contain my joy.

"And you will sit all day, every day, reviewing resumés from assholes like you who don't seem to realize they lack the skills necessary to wipe their own asses, much less work here."

He loved me!

When I arrived the next day I was shown to a cubicle where I would sit, day after day, reading and evaluating resumés -- "from assholes just like me" -- to see if any of them fit the list of job openings that was delivered to my desk each morning.

Few of them did.

After about three months of this, just as I was preparing to throw the six or seven hundred resumés we had received that week out the window and then jump out after them, I was given a new piece of paper.

"This is highly confidential," I was told. "There are three executive openings within the company, and the president wants to interview each finalist personally."

For a moment, I imagined the president coming down and sitting in my little cubicle to page through a stack of resumés until he found the candidates he was looking for -- but then I realized I was expected to find the right candidates.

"You are not to use the inter-office mail for this search. When you have found the right candidates, you are to walk the resumés to the president's office yourself. His office is on the fifth floor."

The fifth floor! I'd never been on the fifth floor. We had twenty floors in our building, and I'd been on all of them -- except for the fifth floor. That was the executive floor, and peons like me were not allowed.

Up until then, I'd never seen any place like the reception area on the fifth floor. It was gigantic -- as big as a hotel lobby -- and it had the thickest carpet I had ever walked on. Beautiful works of art adorned the walls.

I approached the desk timidly, just as Oliver approached the overseer for more gruel. An elegantly dressed mature woman sat at the reception desk with her hands folded neatly. She greeted me with a smile. When I explained why I was there, she gestured -- not with her finger, but with her whole hand -- to large glass doors across the room. "Just over there," she said. Her voice was quiet and elegant — and British.

Two secretaries sat side-by-side and both looked up when I entered the next office. Matching vases of tulips sat on a corner of each desk, which was notable because it was the dead of winter. I announced the purpose of my visit -- "I am from Employee Relations," I stammered, "and I have some resumés for the president to review."

"Yes, of course," one of them -- a pretty blonde -- said, as she picked up a phone and pushed a button. She was soft spoken, so I couldn't make out her words, but she soon hung up and said, "Go right in, Mr. John," as she pointed to a wall across the room.

I walked over to what appeared to be a double-wide door covered with the same rich fabric that covered the walls. There was no doorknob, so I turned around with a helpless look on my face. "Just place your hand on that square panel to the right," the blonde said.

I did, and both doors whisked open electrically. I walked into the most magnificent office I'd ever seen. The president was there, sitting at an enormous desk, but he didn't look up. Finally he realized I was standing there and stood, extending his hand as he introduced himself. I told him my name and that I was from Employee Relations as I handed him the confidential envelope and prepared to beat an exit.

"Sit," he commanded, gesturing to a chair lest I might misunderstand and just drop in a heap on the floor.

I sat. He opened the envelope and went through the five resumés I had chosen for him.

"Excellent," he said. He picked three out of the pile and handed them back to me. "Get these guys in here for an interview. Karen will tell you when I'm available." I was dismissed.

I floated from the fifth floor as though I had just been in the presence of God. (I would learn soon enough that, in our company, I wasn't far off.) I returned to my cubicle on the twelfth floor. My floor was nice enough: it had a decent industrial-weight carpet, nice-enough prints on the walls, plants here and there, and overhead fluorescent lighting. But I had been Cinderella for a few minutes, and now it was time to mop the floors.

I wondered if I would ever see the fifth floor again.

I did. I got to know the company president from my recurring visits to the fifth floor. We weren't drinking buddies or anything like that, but it wasn't unusual to receive a call from him telling me to look for a candidate to fill a particular job. He seemed to like my choices, and several of them were hired. My visits to the fifth floor were becoming more frequent, but I was still in awe every time the elevator doors opened.

As I was leaving his office one day, he stopped me before I reached the door.

"Rex, how would you like a new job?" he asked.

So. It had come to that. I knew this is how they phrased things on the fifth floor. Instead of saying, "Beat it -- you're fired," they said things like, "We've been thinking you might be happier elsewhere...."

I froze, trying to imagine what I had done to make him unhappy. But I didn't want to burn this bridge; even a short stint in this company would look good on my resumé. So, I gulped and tried to smile as I said, "Well, I will be sorry to leave, Sir. I've actually enjoyed my time here very much, and I appreciate having had the opportunity to work for your company."

He looked puzzled for a second and then laughed aloud. "No, Rex. Not a new job somewhere else -- a new job here, in *this* company!"

I'm sure I let out a sigh of relief but all I said was,

"Oh....yes....well....yes....of course....that would be nice.
…"

I could tell he was already beginning to question his own judgment when he said, "Okay then, we'll get back to you."

I was dismissed again.

When I returned to my twelfth floor cubicle this time, I wondered what he meant by a "new job." I was already as low in the company as I could go. Other than two housekeepers on the fifth floor, who spent the whole day serving coffee to upper level executives and tidying up, I didn't know of any job below mine. My job as clerk was only one grade level above theirs -- and one of them actually made more money than I did because she had been there for so long. I knew these things because I had access to everybody's payroll information.

But I also knew there weren't many other jobs in the company that didn't require specialized training. It had already been established that I wasn't a geologist or engineer or oil and gas accountant, which left only secretarial-type jobs. I wondered how I would do as a male secretary in a company where secretaries were still "encouraged" to wear dresses or skirts. I didn't even own a skirt. Would I have to start cross-dressing? I'd never done that (if you don't count the nurse's outfit I was forced to wear as a child) and I didn't think I'd like it.

A new stack of resumés was waiting for me when I reached my desk, so I had to put my musings aside and get to work. The president had said "they would get back to me," so I'd just have to wait and see what happened.

I didn't have to wait long.

About three o'clock in the afternoon, a kid from the

Office Services department came around the corner of my cubicle pushing a two-wheeled cart.

"Are you Mr. John?" he asked.

I looked at him and noted that he was about my age, if not a year or two older.

"Yes, I'm Rex," I said.

"Okay. Well, I've been told to come help you pack up your desk."

I looked at him again, then I looked around my cubicle. I had a coffee cup, a sack lunch sitting on one end of my desk and two small photos of my wife and kids tacked to the bulletin board. My coat hung on a coat rack in the corner.

I smiled at him and said, "Um, there's not much to pack up. I think I can manage by myself, thanks."

He puzzled over this, obviously expecting to fill the three empty boxes on his cart. "Well, okay. I guess you should just come with me then. They told me where to take you."

This ought to be good, I thought. "Maybe I should just tell my supervisor where I'm going...," I said, but before I got the words out, she popped around the corner.

"So you got promoted, eh?" She sounded happy for me. "Well, good for you. Good luck then," and with that she was gone.

I looked helplessly at the Office Services kid and shrugged. "Okay, I guess I'm ready."

He shrugged, too, and pushed his dolly toward the elevators. Unsure about what was expected, I waited as he pushed the button and then followed him into the elevator when it arrived. He didn't look at me, but I watched as he pushed the button for the fifth floor.

The fifth floor? Why? Which secretary's cubicle was vacant on the fifth floor? Where were they going to put me -- in the executive dining room, helping the maids? But before I could get too worked up, we arrived on the fifth floor, and he wheeled his cart out, obviously expecting me to follow him. I did.

By this time the receptionist knew me, since I was up on "her" floor every few days -- and she greeted me by name. I smiled and said, "Hello."

She said, "Congratulations, by the way."

"Thanks," I said, wondering if everybody knew about my new job but me.

The kid steered toward the president's office but took a quick turn to the right just before we reached it. Instead, we went around a corner to a beautiful office with floor-to-ceiling windows overlooking Denver's busy 17th Street -- the "Wall Street of The West." The office was furnished with a large desk, bookshelves, a credenza and two guest chairs. Other than that, it was empty.

"Well, here you go," the kid said, like he'd just dropped off a child at daycare.

I sat in the guest chair nearest the door wondering what was happening. This had to be some kind of mistake. I had just been dropped off on the executive floor -- the *fifth* floor -- and I was now seated in a private office with big windows. Why? What was I supposed to do next?

Moments later, there was a knock on the door and a lovely young woman appeared. "Hello, I'm Stephanie, Mr. John. I've been assigned as your secretary."

Well, that's a relief! I may not have known *what* I'd be doing but at least now I knew *who* would be doing it.

She was soon joined by another woman, this one

middle-aged, who introduced herself as Dottie and indicated she would be assisting Stephanie as she assisted me.

Oh good! Now there are three of us to do whatever it is I'm supposed to be doing.

"Um, ladies," I said, gesturing to the guest chairs and closing the door. "There's only one problem. I don't even know why I'm here. I don't even know what my job is. I think I've been promoted, but I don't know for sure."

They smiled, and I could see that they found me amusing, because they had already been told what was going on. I realized they knew much more than I did. I would eventually discover that would always be the case.

"You are the new Director of Community Relations," one of them said. "You are responsible for corporate philanthropy and representing our company with the non-profit organizations who come to us for help."

That sounded interesting, if only because I wouldn't have to pretend that I was a geologist.

"Who's been doing the job until now?" I asked.

"Well, that's just it. Nobody," the other one said. "The top executives just sort of do their own thing and give out money to whoever asks. But the president wants that to stop. He wants a more thoughtful approach to where and how we help the community -- and he thinks you're the man to do it."

I was dumbfounded. The man hardly knew me at all. I was humbled that he thought I was capable of doing such an important job.

Getting an office on the fifth floor and two wonderful secretaries to help me, along with a new job with a big-shot title, wasn't the only surprise coming my way. I didn't know it that day, but my next paycheck revealed that I had received a 300 percent raise in one day -- and many more substantial increases and bonuses came in the months and years to come.

Stephanie and Dottie eventually went back to their desks, and I moved across the room to sit at mine for the first time. I walked over and looked out the huge window on the bustle of 17th Street, and I marveled at my good fortune. I knew then that some people must climb the corporate ladder the hard way, hand over fist and others, like me, apparently just take the elevator.

The Great Underwear Flap

In 1977 a man named Roy Raymond went to buy underwear for his wife in a department store.

Some people will read that sentence and say, "Yeah, sure." Wink. Wink. But it's true. There really was a Roy Raymond and, as far as I know he wasn't a cross-dresser or transvestite. And according to Wikipedia, Mr. Raymond really did go to a department store to buy underwear for his wife -- but found it to be an "unpleasant experience." Most straight men would probably concur -- which may be why most of them would never agree to such a thing in the first place.

That's their loss.

It turns out that Mr. Raymond was so embarrassed that he went home and started his own business selling -- what else -- ladies underwear. That store today is known as Victoria's Secret. Five years after Mr. Raymond's unpleasant experience, he was grossing $6 million a year, which presumably cured his embarrassment.

One wonders why he was embarrassed in the first place. I mean, it's just underwear, right? Maybe he thought it was too out in the open -- too impersonal. If so, he certainly took care of the problem in his Victoria's Secret stores. I will admit that I haven't spent much time in Victoria's Secret, but I am told it is a comfortable place for men to shop because the female sales staff are eager to assist these poor guys by helping them estimate the "approximate size" of their wife or girlfriend.

Um....okay....

And just how does she do that, I wonder. I can imagine a clerk holding up her breasts for a male customer and saying, "Is she about this big?"

"Um...I'm not sure just by looking...," he would probably answer.

"Well, here, give me your hands," she might say.

And that, folks, is why Victoria's Secret has grown to more than 1,000 stores in the United States, causing one to wonder how on earth women got their underwear before men started buying it for them.

Don't hold your breath for a similar store designed for men's undergarments. For one thing, the great majority of men have no secrets. Most guys would be more than happy to whip out whatever it is you want to see. Second, until very recently, all guys' underwear was divided into two simple categories: grabbers or hangers. That doesn't offer a lot of choice. For the unenlightened, by the way, "grabbers" are also known as "tighty-whities" -- Jockey shorts. "Hangers" are what we used to call "old man" underwear -- baggy boxers. That is no longer the case, since most young guys now wear hangers, just like their grandfathers did.

Most boys are born into one kind of underwear culture, and stay that way for their entire lives. If his dad wore grabbers, so does he. If he wore boxers, the kid does too.

That alone is noteworthy. For most of history, men weren't allowed to decide much about their new-born children -- that was the mother's job. But for some reason, men are allowed to decide what kind of underwear their little knock-off will wear. (We are also allowed to weigh-in on circumcision -- whether the kid will be "cut" or "un-cut" -- but that, too, usually follows the example of the dad.)

I wore Jockey shorts -- tighty-whities -- from the beginning. (Well, I may have spent a few days in diapers, but I'm sure I was potty-trained early. They say kids who are potty-trained too early suffer from frazzled nerves. That's my proof.)

My dad wore tighty-whities, so that's what they put me in. That's all there was to it. When my mom went to buy underwear for one of us, she usually bought them for both of us. I was in college before I discovered that new underwear didn't just appear in my drawer automatically.

I will say this for tighty-whities: you always know exactly where everything is.

Even so, when I was in my early thirties I noticed an ad for boxers that made them look sexy -- not like "old men underwear." I decided I might need to try a pair just to see what they were like.

So, the next time I was in a downtown department store where I occasionally ate lunch (nicer department stores had lunchrooms back then -- sort of like the hot dog stands at Target or Costco these days, only with appetizing food) and while walking through the men's department, I saw a display of boxer shorts. I looked through the available styles and colors and chose what I considered to be a nice-looking three-pack. I made sure they were in my waist size but neglected to note the description "slim guy cut."

Nobody has ever accused me of being a "slim guy."

The next day when I dressed for work, I put a pair on and looked at myself in the mirror. Then I looked at the photo on the package before looking in the mirror again. If I hadn't been in my own bedroom, I would have sworn I was staring into a fun house mirror -- the wavy kind that made tall and thin people look short and fat or, in this case, just the opposite.

I was a stud.

On my way to the office that morning I had to stop for a breakfast meeting. That's where I first noticed, as I was walking into the restaurant, that the "horse," as they say, had gotten out of the "barn."

Nobody else could see this, of course, but it was a bit more daring than I like to be. I wasn't one of those guys who had no qualms about going "commando" when they ran out of clean underwear. I always wore underwear whether they were clean or not.

Just kidding. They were always clean.

But this day, they were also malfunctioning. I made a side-trip into the men's room where I put everything back in place before meeting my guest.

Later, as I was walking through the ornate lobby of the downtown building where I worked, I realized it had happened again. The horse seemed determined to enjoy his new-found freedom, and kept popping out through the rather loose barn door. And even though nobody else knew what was going on, it was annoying to me.

As I walked through the lobby, I glanced around to see

who might be getting in the elevator with me. If I was alone, I planned to turn it into my own private dressing room.

The only person in sight was the guard on duty at the lobby desk, and based on my previous interactions with him, I could have turned the elevator into a rocket to the moon and he wouldn't have cared.

As soon as I got in the elevator, I pushed the button for my floor and jammed my hand down the front of my pants to make the necessary adjustment. But just as the doors were closing, four fingers with bright red finger nail polish slid between them, causing them to fly back open. The fingers, it turned out, were attached to a hand which was attached to an arm which was attached to a no-nonsense looking woman in a smart-looking suit and high heels. She stepped in, and the doors were finally allowed to close.

I had a problem. I stood there with my hand down the front of my pants, halfway up to my elbow. If I moved too quickly to withdraw it, it would obviously give away what I had been doing -- and make me look like a pervert. So I left my hand right where it was, grateful that I wasn't wearing see-through pants. I probably looked like Napoleon -- that is, if Napoleon had stuck his hand in his pants instead of the front of his coat.

She turned and stared at me, as if daring me to do something kinky. I looked straight ahead -- refusing to meet her gaze, and kept my hand right where it was. I was hoping she would think that's where I always kept it. I could feel my face heating up though, and I'm sure I was bright red. She continued to stare, and I continued to ignore her, until we came to the fifth floor which, mercifully, was my stop. I got off and withdrew my hand from its hiding place.

My horse was probably laughing his head off.

Mr. Francy Pants

Brad recently bought some underwear by mail. At first I thought that was kind of weird, until I remembered that you can't try on underwear in the store anyway -- thank goodness, because I'd rather not put on a pair of underwear that somebody else has been wearing. So why not buy by mail?

I sometimes tease Brad about having an underwear fetish, but that's just because I'm jealous that his skivvies are so much nicer than mine. I buy underwear by the three-pack at an outlet store. They are white and have what is euphemistically referred to (by the manufacturer) as a "kangaroo pouch." (My "kangaroo" says 'huh?') But Brad buys his underwear one pair at a time, for twenty-five bucks and up, and they all seem to be designer originals -- colorful patterns and varying fabrics, all smartly tailored -- but lacking -- too bad for him -- a "kangaroo pouch."

I'll say it again: I think if you spend $25 for one pair of underwear, you have a fetish.

One time, when we were in France, I said I had a

craving for pizza (nothing unusual about that) and he responded by saying, "I need some underwear." I didn't quite see the connection, but we headed off to the store -- which happened to be right down the street from a pizza parlor.

As we walked, I gingerly tried to bring up the subject of his obsession with underwear.

Finally I said, "Why don't you just throw your underwear away, like I do?" I asked.

"What are you talking about?" he said, no doubt wishing I'd go back to talking about pizza.

"Well, this is a trick my friend Mike taught me. I save up my underwear all year, and when a pair just gets too raggedy to wear anymore, I put it aside for our next trip. Then, on the trip, I wear the pair one last time and chuck it in the trash."

"No wonder you feel compelled to leave such big tips for the hotel maids," he said. "And it may not be enough, now that I think about it."

"Yes, but it works," I said. "Then I have more room in my suitcase for things I buy on the trip."

"You mean like underwear," he said as we turned into his favorite clothing shop, a place called Celio. He bought his new underwear, and I spent the whole time trying to ask the salesperson, in my fractured French, if they sold pizza.

Back in our apartment later that day, he came into the living room modeling one of the new pairs of underwear he'd bought -- a bikini cut affair, in some kind of animal print. They were so out of character on him I almost burst out laughing.

"Well, look at you," I exclaimed. "Mister Francy

Pants!"

Brad is shy by nature, so other than walking into the living room in his underwear (fortunately, we didn't have dinner guests) he didn't want the spotlight to linger too long. "These are my Celio underwear," he said sheepishly.

Well, I'd completely forgotten about the shopping trip and the name of the store, Celio, so I thought he said, "These are my silly 'ole underwear."

So I said the first thing that popped into my head: "They certainly are!"

To be fair, Brad comes by this underwear obsession naturally.

Based on a story his late mother told me, it is entirely possible that he was named for a brand of men's underwear.

This story came out when he and I were having dinner with his mother, June, a few years ago. By that time she was getting somewhat frail, and not every restaurant was appealing to her. One of her favorites, but not necessarily ours, was the Olive Garden -- possibly because it was easier to get in and out of than some of the other, fancier restaurants we might have chosen.

To get an idea of what Brad thinks of the Olive Garden, all you need to know is that he refers to houses that are decorated in any rustic Tuscan style as being "Early Olive Garden."

The only response I have to that is: Hot Artichoke Spinach Dip.

Anyway, we were at the Olive Garden and I was trying to get his mother to talk, which was one of my assigned duties.

"June," I said, "I'm curious about Brad's name. Where did you get it? Is he named after an old friend, or a relative, or a cowboy star?"

That last part was a private joke. I don't know of any cowboy stars named "Brad," but since my mother had the questionable taste to name me after "Rex Allen, the Singing Cowboy," I figure it doesn't hurt to ask.

A few minutes earlier, when we were about to order our entrees, I had teasingly asked Brad what he was going to get by saying, "What looks good to you, Dr. Snyder?"

Apparently I'd called him "Dr. Snyder" more than once, because his mother snapped: "Why do you keep calling him that? He's not a doctor!"

I was taken back but regained my composure quickly enough to say, "Well, he is too. He earned his Ph.D. -- and he worked hard at it -- so that means he's earned the honorific of 'doctor' once in a while, even if he's not an M.D."

I don't remember what she said after that, but I think it was something like "Oh, pshaw!" before she went back to studying the menu.

Minutes later I worried that I would raise her ire again by my question about how he got his name. I waited.

She seemed to be struggling for an answer, and for a moment I wondered if she would even be able to remember. I imagined the thought process in her head as she gazed at her son: "Who is this man and why does he think he is a doctor?"

Finally she nodded and smiled as if remembering.

"Well," she said, "my husband had asked me to go shopping a few weeks before my due date and he gave me a list which included new underwear for him. I went downtown to the department store, and while I was walking through the men's section, I noticed a display for a new swimsuit called 'The Bradley.'"

And that was it. She stopped, as though that was the end of the story.

I sat there, gape-jawed, trying to absorb what I'd just heard.

"Now let me get this straight," I said. "Are you saying that you named your son after a *swimsuit?*"

"Yes," she said. "A swimsuit."

I was incredulous. I remembered the machinations my wife and I went through to find names for our children -- agonizing over lists and lists of boy baby and girl baby names, from Banjo and Zane to Ursula and Muffin -- afraid of making the wrong decision lest our kids grow up to be psychopaths and smother us in our beds. We polled our parents, grandparents and all of our friends. "Which name do you like best?" we asked, wanting to make sure our final choice met with everybody's approval. Now this woman was telling me she named her handsome, brilliant son after an article of clothing in the men's department!

After allowing this new information to settle for a moment, I turned to Brad and said, "Well! I guess we can be glad your mother didn't see the Speedo display first!"

But at that moment, thanks to his mother, Brad got a new nickname, which I call him to this day: Speedo -- or, if I'm feeling feisty, "Doctor" Speedo.

Would "Apnea" Be a Good Girl's Name?

One of my favorite movie scenes is from "Send Me No Flowers," starring Rock Hudson and Doris Day. As I recall, the two -- husband and wife -- were in the midst of a marital spat just before bedtime. Foolishly thinking the fight was over, Rock falls asleep, which infuriates Doris. After watching him snore for a few minutes, she slaps him across the face so hard his head bounces off the pillow. He bolts upright and, rubbing his cheek, stammers, "Wha...what happened?"

Doris pretends she's been asleep and says, "Hmmm? What darling? What's wrong? Did you have a bad dream?"

This happens to me practically every night.

No, Doris Day doesn't slap me across the face, but she might as well, because I simply cannot sleep through the night.

It may be that I fear sleep. I have tried to analyze this and, as far as I know, I'm not afraid of the dark, or of monsters under the bed, or anything like that. The best I can come up with is that I worry about sleeping with my mouth open, which means bugs could fly in and set up housekeeping. ("Look at how big this room is, dear...I can lay my eggs right over there, behind that gold-covered tooth....")

To counter this, each night when I get in bed, I spend about ten minutes pounding the pillow into submission. Then I carefully position the palm of my right hand under my chin to hold my mouth shut. It's never there when I wake up, of course, which makes me worry that my mouth has been hanging wide open all night. This fear, combined with the fact that it is extremely dry in Colorado, means that I often can't swallow when I first wake up. When I complained about this to Brad not long ago, asking him why my mouth was so dry he said, "Probably moths."

Like many older people, I have recently begun having "sleep issues." Brad is the notable exception to this rule, even though he is eight years older than I am. When he goes to bed, he is asleep before I can count to twenty -- and I am not exaggerating. He also has the annoying habit of sleeping soundly through the night.

This is the complete opposite of when I was in my twenties, thirties and forties. Back then I actually worried that I was narcoleptic. I slept all over the place: in movies, before the movie even began (and certainly in the middle of it), in church (for obvious reasons), in class, at work, and even in the car. I once drove off the highway going 60 miles an hour with three of my cousins in the car. (They were all asleep, so why shouldn't I be, I reasoned.)

But then, like Rip Van Winkle, I woke up -- and I've stayed awake ever since.

A few years ago I became so distressed about my

inability to sleep that I sought the help of my doctor. He happened to be an attractive young man, very doctorly, so I secretly hoped he would simply come over every night and read to me until I fell asleep.

Instead, he arranged for me to be tested for "apnea," which is a sleep disorder characterized by interrupted breathing. When you stop breathing, he explained, you wake up.

Stupid me. I thought when you stopped breathing you died. Turns out that you simply wake up. That may come as a surprise to all the people who stopped breathing and are now buried six feet under ground.

The doctor arranged for me to spend a night at a sleep clinic at one of our most prestigious hospitals in order to sleep under observation.

Oh sure. I couldn't help but wonder why, if I complained that I couldn't sleep, he thought I would be able to do so while being "observed." I could envision a situation where whoever was watching me just sat there for eight hours while I played possum so I wouldn't feel like I was wasting their time.

I reported for duty about 8 o'clock on the appointed night and was placed in a badly furnished room. Oh well, I thought, if I can't sleep at least I can get up and redecorate.

The nurse informed me that the room was sound-proof, which proved to be true. It was so quiet, in fact, that I could hear the blood pounding against my temples.

I was told to undress and get into the bed at which time she would return to attach the monitoring devices. I did so, but not before noticing that there was a large one-way mirror on one side of the room. I assume the nurse and probably the night janitor were waiting on the other side for me to start stripping.

The so-called "monitoring devices" turned out to be a little less comfortable than one might think. Here is a little demonstration which will enable you to get a sense of what was involved. First, you will need about ten extension cords and a roll of duct tape.

Using the duct tape, tape the ends of all ten wires (it doesn't matter which end, this is just an illustration) to various places all over your head and face. Just for fun, tape a few to each shoulder and maybe one or two just below your knees.

Comfy?

Never mind, get in bed. But before you start scratching and playing with everything you usually scratch and play with when you get under the covers, you should wave goodnight to the people across the room who are watching you through the glass. (If you are trying this experiment in your own home, roll your bed up under your living room window and leave the curtains open -- and the light on -- all night. Perhaps some strangers will come up to the window and watch you.)

Sleepy? No? Well, neither was I.

And yet, miraculously, I soon fell sound asleep and, presumably, continued breathing. Until I stopped.

But then I started again.

And then I stopped.

But then...well, you get the idea.

The next morning the "sleep technician," as she had apparently re-named herself during the night, showed me a computer print-out of my "sleep patterns" for the previous six hours. I had no idea which way was up on the paper, and certainly not what any of the lines meant. But I did know I hadn't slept well.

I was sent back to talk to my doctor who, having undergone eight years of medical school, sat me down and solemnly announced that, based on the sleep study, I wasn't sleeping well.

Before I could remind him that I had, in fact, determined that on my own, he confirmed his earlier diagnosis: I had sleep apnea.

I had to marvel at the medical breakthroughs that have occurred over time which allowed me to take part in such an important scientific study and to benefit from such a highly technical diagnosis. And all this for a mere two thousand dollars, which was the price of my "sleep study."

The solution, the doctor explained, was for me to spend an additional $1,500 for a piece of equipment called a CPAP machine and attach it to my face every night when I go to bed. CPAP, according to Wikipedia, stands for "Continuous Positive Airway Pressure." In other words, a machine that forces you to breathe whether you want to or not.

Unless you've been diagnosed with sleep apnea, it is possible that you have never heard of this type of machine, so I will illustrate how it works. You will need a length of garden hose attached to a large zip-lock bag. Put the bag over your head and seal the opening around the end of the garden hose. You should put the other end of the hose in front of a fan (an oscillating room fan will be fine) and then have your spouse or partner jump on the hose every ten or fifteen seconds to stop and re-start the flow of air into your bag. He or she should make a noise each time he jumps (maybe pound the bottom of a kitchen pan with a wooden spoon). Now you know what to expect from your new CPAP machine.

Nighty night!

I didn't buy the machine. That alone is out of character for me. If a doctor or dentist prescribes something, I usually do it -- and I have a whole drawer of mouth appliances to prove it. (I also grind my teeth at night. I'm telling you, it's like the *Nitty Gritty Dirt Band* around here.) A rubber mouth protector supposedly prevents teeth grinding, but I always stop using it when I become paranoid that I am going to swallow it and choke to death.

When I told a friend that I had been diagnosed with sleep apnea and that a CPAP machine had been prescribed, but that I didn't want to get it, he suggested I ask my doctor about alternative treatments.

I had a better idea. I found another doctor.

The next doctor prescribed sleeping pills which, I reasoned, are easier to swallow than, say, a rubber mouth guard. When I filled the prescription, I noticed that it was an awfully large bottle -- about the size of a tennis ball can -- so I was somewhat dismayed to discover that there were only five little pills inside. Apparently my new doctor wanted me to sleep soundly -- but not for more than a week.

The doctor may not have known it, but as it turned out, each pill actually lasted about a week. The first time I took one I slept from ten o'clock at night until two o'clock the next afternoon. Even after I woke up, I walked around like a zombie until nine o'clock that night when I decided it was time for bed again. The bottle warned me against "driving or operating heavy machinery," which wasn't a problem since I could barely find the energy to flush the toilet.

I can't decide which is worse: lying awake all night or allowing myself to fall asleep knowing full well that spiders and moths will begin nesting in my open mouth.

Maybe I'll just take another pill.

Pigging Out

When I was traveling in Spain a number of years ago, a friend and I found ourselves in an elegant restaurant in Seville as guests of the Spanish Tourist Board.

We weren't permitted to order from the menu ("Could I just have the *churros con chocolate*, please?") but were brought dish after dish of local specialties as selected by our hosts. To this day I can remember the paella served in a pan as big as a wading pool, in which the smell of saffron was so strong it almost knocked me from here to next door, which is France, and where I would have said, "Could I just have a *crème brûlée*, please?"

The highlight of the dinner was the presentation of the main dish, *lechón* -- roast suckling pig. I saw the animal coming at me from across the room, carried high on the shoulders of two waiters, flying through the air on an enormous plank of wood. It's true: pigs do fly.

A few minutes earlier I was blissfully unaware of why the waiter was clearing a large piece of real estate on the tablecloth in front of me -- I assumed he was making it easier for me to pass out on the table from the gallons of sangria we were drinking. I was hoping the next thing he would bring would be an overstuffed pillow.

But instead he brought an overstuffed pig.

From the fanfare accompanying this presentation, I knew enough not to run retching from the room. I would find out later that this was a good move on my part and no doubt contributed to world peace, as the Spaniards take their roast pigs very seriously. It was supposed to be an enormous compliment that this blackened, hairy corpse had been placed directly in front of me, its glassy eyes looking up longingly, its snout so close that if he'd had a runny nose I would have needed a tissue in my lap. And let's not forget the big apple stuffed in its mouth -- his eyes trying to tempt me to engage in a no-hands game of "who can eat the most until we meet in the center?"

Well, I ain't kissin' no pigs.

I don't remember how that evening ended -- thank goodness for sangria -- but I'm pretty sure I simply moved around on my plate whatever was served to me from that point forward.

Don't misunderstand. I have absolutely no qualms about eating pork. Bacon? It's my middle name. Hot dogs? Plain, with relish and mustard, please. Barbecued pork? Pile it high.

Let's just say I am not a vegetarian.

But I really don't like my food looking me in the eye while I'm eating it. For example, I ask that the head of trout be removed before it is served. Ditto for lambs, cows and lobsters. Having the whole head of a pig six inches from my face was 200 feet too close for comfort.

I had managed to block out that encounter with Porky Pig until yesterday, when a Facebook posting of an acquaintance brought it all back in living color.

It seems this friend had recently attended a fundraising event for an animal protection organization. The party had a South Pacific theme and included a luau -- a luau in which a barbecued pig was the guest of honor.

Now I'm not an expert in such things, but I must say this seems like a no-brainer. Why would an organization purporting to love animals slaughter one for dinner? Moreover, why would they display it with its piggy eyes, snout and apple-stuffed mouth on the buffet table?

Apparently I wasn't alone in questioning the wisdom of the menu. Within hours, my friend's original Facebook entry had more than 100 sputtering expressions of outrage, most of which included a solemn promise never to send money to the organization again. Oink!

And why should they? I agree, and I don't even own an animal!

Wait, animal lovers! Don't stop reading! I may not be an animal lover, but I *am* an animal *liker* -- and I like some of them very much. For example, when I see my neighbors walking their dogs (forty neighbors, 2,000 dogs), I always stop to pet them. (The dogs, not the neighbors.) And I always ask before touching their pets, not so much out of politeness as fear -- since I almost lost a digit to a testy little mutt who didn't like my looks. (Truth be told, the feeling was mutual and I think he knew it.) As further proof that I do not dislike animals, I am allergic to cats but I can't resist petting them for hours after they climb into my lap and refuse to budge until I've petted them for hours. Isn't that worth a few days of swollen, watery eyes and big red welts all over my arms?

As a child, I owned three dogs successively: Buffer,

Trixie, and Bubbles -- all goofy dogs (and, I hasten to add, named by others) -- and, of course, I loved them: they were my dogs!

But animals belonging to other people? Meh. But if it's any consolation, I feel the same way about other people's children.

The truth is, I think that some people -- not all -- take the animal thing a bit far.

In 2011, Americans spent almost $51 *billion* on their pets. True, pets need food and occasional trips to the vet, but in my opinion, the pet pedicures and diamond-studded dog collars? Please.

Some pet owners disagree with me -- the late Leona Helmsley, for example. Mrs. Helmsley, the oft-referred to "Queen of Mean" for the way she treated her employees (who did not have the good sense to be born dogs), left her Maltese dog $12 million in her will. A man in North Carolina left $2 million to local cats, and only a few years ago, three Chihuahuas living in Miami were embroiled in a battle over a $3 million trust fund.

I do not hate animals. The truth is, I probably like pets more than I like a lot of their owners.

That's why I'd like to clear up some confusion about a dinner years ago during which I may have made eight life-long enemies.

My wife and I were attending a black-tie event to raise money for a new aquarium at our local zoo. I was working for a company that supported every good cause in the community, and probably everybody agrees that a zoo is a good community resource. My company bought two tickets to this particular event and asked me to represent them. It was an odd evening in several respects, beginning with the fact that we were seated at a table with eight strangers. This was unusual back then, as we knew a lot of people and a lot of people knew us. In fact, we knew dozens of people who were attending the event that night -- just not the eight with whom we had been seated.

People who don't know me well are always surprised to hear that I am quite shy. This can be a problem, because when I am feeling shy or out of my element, I tend to talk too much and try too hard.

So, as soon as we were seated, I began trying to make conversation. I began by reading aloud the printed menu that appeared at each of our places. I'm sure I sounded like a first-grader "Hooked on Phonics," but I couldn't help myself.

You can imagine my surprise when I got to the main course listed on the menu -- fish. I don't recall what kind of fish it was, only that it was the kind that had eyes, a mouth and fins and had lived in the water when it was alive. In other words, the kind of fish that might live in an aquarium -- maybe even the kind of aquarium we were trying to build.

"Can this be true?" I asked the strangers. "We're having *fish* for dinner tonight?"

They stared at me blankly.

"Aren't we here to raise money for a new *aquarium*?" I asked, my incredulity shown by the tone (and volume) of my voice.

Still nothing.

"Fish! We're eating fish tonight when we're here to save them!"

Finally, some mealy-mouthed socialite across the table piped up and said, "So, what's wrong with that?"

"I hope you're kidding," I snapped. "Does that mean if we were here to raise money for a new elephant house, we'd be eating elephant tonight? And what about the monkeys? When the zoo decides to build a new monkey habitat, will we be eating monkeys for dinner? I hear they're quite tasty...."

Now I was on a roll and couldn't have been stopped, even if my wife had stabbed me in the leg with her fork which she later told me she dearly wanted to do. "I have an idea!" I said, "Let's eat all the animals in the zoo -- then we won't have to support it anymore!"

After that, we ate our fish in silence, nobody daring to include us in any of their conversations.

Animal lovers.

About Those Yellow Stockings

Everybody has a favorite aunt and many people have a crazy aunt. In my case, I have a couple of each.

Aunt Agnes -- and I know that sounds like a name you'd make up for a crazy aunt, but it was actually her real name -- was my father's sister. He had four other sisters and seven brothers for a total of thirteen children. With that many kids, one of them is bound to be a bit wacky, and that certainly describes Aunt Agnes. The others were just crazy.

Since my dad was the youngest boy in this bunch, I suspect he endured more than his share of bullying. And that may explain why I am an only child.

My mother died when I was five years old, and I was sent to live with my paternal grandparents. These are the same people who had just finished raising the thirteen children ("Whew!" I can imagine them saying as the door closed on the last one) when my dad dropped me on their doorstep. My memory may be foggy on this, but I don't recall anybody throwing confetti as I toddled in the front door.

My grandmother was exhausted, understandably, but not too tired to hold me on her lap and read to me every day until I learned to read myself, at which time I held her on my lap and read to her. It was all quite cozy. My grandfather was livid -- also understandable, given the circumstances -- and I don't recall him saying a word to me my whole life. As far as I know he was capable of speech, he just didn't waste it on a snot-nosed five-year-old he never wanted in the first place.

As a bonus for everybody, shortly after I arrived, Aunt Agnes showed up. Nobody has ever told me this, but I suspect one of the other aunts or uncles wrote her a letter and told her to come home immediately to help care for me. (Apparently I required a great deal of effort and attention.) She had been a nurse in the mission field in South America -- bandaging the natives' injuries while trying to save their souls.

I don't have many memories of those early years, but I remember the day Aunt Agnes arrived at my grandparents' house. She immediately moved me out of my room (so she could have it) and into a much less desirable space at the back of the house. It didn't have heat and had a closet that doubled as a refrigerator. I don't know how many years it took me to realize it was the kitchen.

Aunt Agnes was the only one of the thirteen siblings who never married, making her the "maiden aunt," as they used to call such women back then. She compensated for the lack of a husband by being bossy, so it wasn't long before she was ordering my grandparents and me around like three misbehaving children.

She didn't like having her orders countermanded,

either. For some reason, she decided early on that my hair was parted on the wrong side. That was easily remedied without having to bother me for an opinion: she merely took a long black comb, wet it, and carved a new part down the other side of my head in much the same way a farmer uses a hoe to furrow a trench in the ground. With a single flick of the wrist, my right-leaning hair was now left-leaning. A king-size dollop of ButchWax sealed everything in place, leaving me looking like the love child of Alfalfa and K.D. Lang.

A few days later my maternal grandmother picked me up for an outing, and the minute I got in the car she said, "What on earth happened to your hair?"

"Aunt Agnes said it was parted on the wrong side," I answered as I felt the top of my head to see if it was still up there.

"Oh, she did, did she?" she said. "Well, we'll just see about that!" And with that, she withdrew a comb from her purse and shoveled my hair back to the other side of my head. Problem solved.

When I returned home a few hours later, Aunt Agnes was aghast. "Who did that to your hair?" she demanded.

"Grandmother," I said, without specifying which one.

"Which grandmother?" she wanted to know.

When I told her it was my mother's mother, she said, "Oh? You mean 'Grandma Boss'?"

Well, I was pretty stupid at that point in my life, so I wouldn't swear that I knew my grandmothers even had last names -- much less what they were. So, when Aunt Agnes referred to her as 'Grandma Boss,' I assumed that was her name. Needless to say, I was disabused of that notion the next time I saw her and said, "Hi, Grandma

Boss!"

I lived with my grandparents -- and Aunt Agnes -- for the next six years, until my dad remarried and came to collect me like a layaway item at K-Mart. But up until that point, there is no question that Aunt Agnes was the dominant influence in my life.

As a nurse, she had acquired certain skills the rest of us didn't have. For example, until she arrived, I made my bed each morning like a good little boy, throwing the covers up toward the head and stuffing my pillow underneath the bedspread. Mission accomplished. (Or sometimes I just stayed in bed and pulled the covers up tight around me and over my head and then slipped out without messing it up.)

None of this would do under Aunt Agnes' oversight. Beds were to be made with hospital corners, and they were torn apart and remade as many times as necessary until those corners were at exactly the correct angle. Shortly after I turned fifty -- and had been out on my own for decades -- I decided nobody could tell me how to make the bed anymore, so I simply tucked the corners in some random fashion as if to say, "Ha! You're not the boss of me!" But then I got up in the middle of the night to re-make the bed. Some habits die hard.

Aunt Agnes was also fanatical about hand-washing. I know this is a skill all children should be taught, so I doubt that my experience was much different than any other kid's. That doesn't mean it annoyed me any less.

A typical conversation at meal time would go like this:

Aunt Agnes: "Did you wash your hands?"

Me: (Petulantly) "Yes."

AA: "Let me see them." (She examines them carefully.)

They're not wet. Why?"

Me: (Sarcastically) "Because I dried them?"

AA: "Go wash them again."

This routine became so predictable that I soon stopped washing them until I'd gone through that first inspection (why wash them twice?) and this, too, was a habit that followed me into adulthood, where I discovered to my chagrin that people weren't going to inspect my hands so I'd better remember to wash them myself before meals.

One day when I was about eight years old (in other words, old enough to know better) Aunt Agnes sent me back to re-wash my hands (which hadn't been washed in the first place) and I realized she'd tricked me. When I got into the bathroom -- we only had one -- I found the sink full of white nylon stockings -- "nurses stockings" -- which were soaking. The water was almost to the top of the sink which would have made it impossible for me to use the sink without (a) causing the water to run over the edge or (b) forcing me to rinse and wring out her stockings and hang them on the wooden rack for this purpose -- something that, in my rebellious state, I wasn't about to do. So, I did the only thing I could think of at that moment. I put the lid of the toilet down, climbed up on top of it, unzipped my pants and peed into the sink. Let her stockings soak in that!

I then washed my hands in the bathtub, which is what I should have done in the first place.

I've never told that story before, for the obvious reason that it makes me look crazy, but Aunt Agnes is no longer with us, so I'm sure she doesn't care. I do remember checking her out over the next few days to see if her stockings looked yellow.

On another occasion, Aunt Agnes decided to teach me about opera. Her teaching technique was to park me in front of the stereo and make me listen to opera records which, for the most part, were sung in Italian or German. After she left the room and I was sure she was occupied elsewhere, I would turn the television on -- with the sound off -- and watch Howdy Doody while Enrico Caruso or Maria Callas provided the soundtrack.

To her credit, Aunt Agnes was always trying to help me become a better boy -- even if that meant putting me in Buster Brown shoes and knee pants, and making me listen to opera. She was like Hyacinth Bucket in the PBS comedy "Keeping Up Appearances," who insisted her name was pronounced "Bouquet." Now that I think of it, Aunt Agnes even looked a bit like Hyacinth, and they certainly shared the same operatic voice inflections.

Aunt Agnes could be unintentionally funny like Hyacinth as well. One conversation stands out vividly in my mind.

We were going somewhere -- to church, probably -- and Aunt Agnes was driving. And because we lived in Colorado where there is virtually no humidity at a mile above sea level, I was picking my nose.

I hasten to point out that this is not only the favorite pastime of an eight-year-old boy, which I was at the time, but also the favorite pastime of almost every citizen of the state of Colorado. You can drive down any street at any time of the night or day and look at the car next to you and see that the driver has one hand on the steering wheel and one finger up his or her nose. That's just the way we roll out here.

Anyway, when Aunt Agnes noticed that I appeared to

be drilling for oil, she said, "Stop that," which naturally caused me to turn, finger still up one nostril, and say, "Stop what?"

"You know what!" she said. "Picking your nose, for heaven's sake. I don't want burgers all over my car."

That's what she said: "burgers."

Well. That got my attention. I slowly withdrew my finger as though if I did it slow enough she wouldn't notice where it had been.

"Burgers?" I said. "Did you say *burgers?* Do you mean 'boogers,' Aunt Agnes?"

"Oh!" she exclaimed in her high-pitched voice. "Don't say that word! It's vulgar."

"Yes, but that's what they're called," I explained as if talking to someone from another country. "Burgers are hamburgers....something you eat."

"Oh!" she shuddered as though I'd suggested she eat my boogers. "Stop it right now! Don't say another word about it!"

And I haven't, until now.

Rest in peace, Aunt Agnes.

Sniff Test

"Smell this," Brad said, holding up what looked like a dirty rag to my nose.

"No, thank-you," I said.

To his credit, he didn't press the point, and my refusal to smell it seemed to confirm his suspicion that the remnant of cloth had been used to polish furniture.

This is one of the many ways in which we differ. Asking me to smell a dirty rag was his way of determining whether it should be saved and repurposed. I, on the other hand, would have simply thrown that rag in the trash and appropriated a new one -- probably one of his Opie shirts -- as a rag.

But Brad should have known better than to ask me to smell anything. I don't smell, as I've repeatedly told him -- one of a long list of items that I don't do, including windows, costume parties, my checkbook, outdoor camping (and rarely indoor camping), hiking uphill (down is okay), eating liver, sleeping on flannel sheets, eating in restaurants that don't take reservations, waiting in lines longer than two people or three minutes, sitting anywhere but on the aisle in movie theaters, flying coach (if I have a choice), and...well, let's just say it's a long list.

Oh, I know *how* to smell -- but I'm not sure that's worth bragging about. I smell things that Brad doesn't -- or says he can't, out of self-protection. In our house I play the role of the canary in the mine shaft. If the house is ever filled with noxious fumes (such as the time I caramelized some onions right through the bottom of the skillet), I will need to be the one who sounds the alarm. We have a carbon monoxide detector, which is required by law, but in our house it goes off whether fumes are present or not -- but only in the middle of the night. The first time it happened I wondered if I was losing my sensitivity to smell. It turns out that it was just a false alarm -- the first of many we would come to enjoy in the months ahead.

But even though I am capable of smell, I choose not to, based on an incident that happened some thirty years ago but is as fresh (smelling) as if it had happened yesterday.

My friend Larry, a prominent attorney in Denver, had come to my office on the top floor of the D&F Tower, an iconic landmark located on the 16th Street Mall in downtown Denver.

It was part social call, part real estate scouting trip for Larry, who was thinking about leasing new office space in the building and had heard about a recently vacated space a few floors below mine. He brought two of his assistants with him after arranging with the building management for me to give them a tour.

I didn't know the assistants, one male and one female, but we chatted cordially on the short elevator trip down to the seventh floor. The vacant office space took up the entire floor, so we stepped off the elevator into the reception area of the former tenant, a law firm.

The place came fully furnished, but it was devoid of any sign that people had ever been there. Rich, dark wood covered the walls and elegant chandeliers hung from the ceiling. The floor was hardwood, scattered with thick oriental rugs.

We walked through the space, commenting on its various attributes. I remember that it had quite a collection of paintings, although they all seemed to have something to do with dogs and hunting. The windows were covered with dark wood shutters and thick velvet draperies which were swagged to each side with a silk cord.

And the desks themselves were old-world traditional, made of solid hardwood with panel insets on the front -- the kind you would expect a powerful attorney to have.

When we returned to the reception area, Larry's male assistant took a seat on the Queen Anne sofa, while his female assistant sat in one of the two leather-covered wingback chairs. Larry sat in the second one and I propped myself on the corner of the receptionist's desk. His secretary soon moved over to the sofa to sit next to her colleague, while the four of us chatted about the suitability of the space.

"I don't know...," he began. "The whole place feels a bit stiff, don't you think?"

Well, that was an understatement. To me, it looked like a mix between a high-end whorehouse and a funeral parlor. I expected Lurch from the Addams family to walk out and offer us mint juleps.

"I kind of like it," the male assistant said, but I had noticed earlier that he was eyeing one of the fancy private offices, so I knew what he was up to.

"And what about this furniture?" Larry asked, looking around the reception area. "Do you think these are antiques? Is this leather real?" he said, patting the arm of the chair in which he was seated.

That's when everything went wrong.

Instead of saying, "Who knows?" as anybody who doesn't know squat about antiques should say, I had to play Mister Know-It-All and offer an opinion.

"Oh, that's easy to tell," I boasted as I jumped off my perch and took several steps toward the vacant chair next to Larry. "Leather is easy. All you have to do is smell it."

So far, so good: the chair was fully covered in leather -- all of it. Anybody with any sense would have bent over and casually smelled the top of the back of the chair...the wing backs...or, although I can't imagine why, the arm rests.

Not me.

I knelt down on the floor as if preparing to say my prayers, and stuck my nose right into the center of the seat cushion -- the same cushion that had held who knows how many butts over the years -- including Larry's secretary, only moments earlier.

As is so often the case when people do something stupid, I realized immediately how absurd this action was. I only hoped Larry and the others hadn't paid any attention.

But they had. By the time I pulled myself back up to a standing position I could see that the mouths of both assistants had dropped open, as if to say, "What the..."

Larry watched me from his chair, much as an amused king might watch the court jester. His mouth was slightly upturned, in what could only be described as a smirk. I silently prayed he would let it pass without comment.

My prayers were not answered.

"Anybody you recognize?" he asked.

And that was how I learned to never use my sense of smell in public.

No More Falsies

I am standing at the door of a McMansion located in one of the tonier sections of Houston. The design of the house is similar, but not identical, to the other houses on the block: nouveau-Georgian, red brick, lots of gables and bright white shutters bracketing the twenty or so windows facing the street.

To reach the front porch, I must walk past a black wrought-iron post with a big ring on it at the end of the sidewalk, presumably placed there to accommodate those who visit on horseback and need a place to tie up their horse. Unfortunately, I have arrived by car.

I eye the doorbell in front of me, but I hesitate to push it. I wonder if it is too late to run. I know this party is going to be horrible, and I hate it already. I had, in fact, made an effort to decline the invitation when it was first issued, but it was what is known in social circles as a "command performance." There are two invitations one supposedly cannot turn down: an invitation from the White House and an invitation from your biggest client -- whose monthly fee pays a large percentage of your overhead.

"Really, Fred," I said when the invitation was issued, "I'd love to come to your birthday party, but I don't do costume parties." Frankly, I can't imagine anybody over the age of eight hosting a costume party for their birthday, but to be fair, Fred's birthday happens to fall on October 31st -- America's newest national holiday: Halloween.

Since Fred had the misfortune of being born on Halloween, his birthday has apparently been celebrated in the form of a costume party his entire life. That would certainly eliminate the possibility of any of his little friends hurting his feelings by not coming to his party, since all his mother would need to do was open the door and drag in a bunch of random trick-or-treaters.

When I told Fred I didn't "do" costume parties, I wasn't quite telling the truth. There had been one notable exception a few years earlier, when I was still in Denver. My friend Dawn had invited me to escort her to what she referred to as a "very exclusive party" being given at the national headquarters of a large corporation. Dawn was a society columnist for one of the two Denver newspapers and often leaned on a cadre of friends to take turns accompanying her to social events around town.

"Is it black tie?" I asked.

"No, it's a costume party," she responded with glee, as if that would seal the deal.

"No, thanks," I said, explaining my policy on costume parties.

Dawn was one of those women who happened to be very persuasive, so before I knew what was happening, I heard myself agreeing to make an exception to my rule "just this once."

"But what should I wear?" I asked. "I don't own any costumes."

"Not a problem," she said. "I already have a costume for you. You can simply change into it when you pick me up."

When I arrived at her house at the appointed time, she was waiting for me at the door in the elaborate dress of a Spanish señorita. It had over-the-top frills and flourishes, so I dreaded finding out what she had planned for me. Eyeing her more closely, I decided it would probably be a flamenco dancer -- with a white puffy-sleeved shirt, a form-fitting black vest and, of course, tight black trousers. A key component of my "look" would surely be shiny black pointy-toed boots, so I wondered how Dawn might have been able to guess my shoe size. The ensemble would, of course, feature a wide silk cummerbund in bright red to match her dress. Olé!

My guess was a little off.

My costume consisted of a Mexican serape -- it looked suspiciously like a beach blanket I'd once bought in Puerto Vallarta -- which Dawn proceeded to sling over my shoulder like a continental soldier. The remainder of the outfit was a sombrero the size of a patio umbrella. That was it.

"No," I said flatly when Dawn brought the two items into her living room.

"Oh, come on!" she said, dragging me out the door. "We'll have so much fun, and with all the elaborate costumes that people will wear, nobody will be looking at you anyway!"

Yeah, right...

The corporate headquarters where the party was being

held had just opened and was rumored to be an architect's and designer's dream. It was billed as "taller than a skyscraper -- on its side." I couldn't wait to see it, costumed or not.

The only problem was, it was located in the foothills some twenty-five miles south of town. To get there it took, according to my rough estimate, forever.

I should have known something was wrong when we pulled up to the front of the building and the tuxedo-clad parking attendants who came to open our doors shot each other a "look." I saw the look, but I wasn't quite sure what it meant. It gave me an uneasy feeling.

As was typical when I went anywhere with Dawn, everybody was already inside. I surrendered the car to an attendant after retrieving my mammoth sombrero from the trunk. Dawn smashed it onto my big head and laughed. That, too, should have been a tip-off.

She took my arm and we strolled to the front door, which two more attendants opened with a flourish. They, too, looked at each other strangely, and I realized in that split second what was going on: we were inappropriately dressed.

Too late. Before I had time to absorb what was happening, we were standing at the top of a stairway leading down dramatically into a grand lobby filled with gentlemen wearing tuxedos and ladies wearing formal gowns.

There wasn't another flamenco dancer in sight, nor anybody dressed in a serape and sombrero.

Apparently Dawn had misunderstood. It wasn't a costume party after all.

She later swore that the party didn't come to a

complete standstill when we entered, as people tried to take in this strangely dressed couple before them. But in my memory, even the band stopped playing...or maybe they started playing the Mexican Hat Dance. It's all a blur.

All I wanted to do was sit down on the step and put my head between my knees, but I realized that would make me look like one of those Mexican ashtrays, the kind you can buy from the vendors on any beach in Acapulco.

Dawn loved it. And as always, she was the life of the party. In her newspaper column the next morning, she gleefully described the whole debacle, pronouncing me "a good sport." I have been grateful from that day to this that I forbade a photographer to take my photo, because I'm sure it would have haunted me for the rest of my life.

That was the sorry day I came up with my "no costume party" rule. So what was I doing standing on Fred's front porch, dressed in a navy-blue skirt, starched white blouse and black cardigan sweater -- all of which covered a gigantic bra stuffed with gym socks? I was also sporting a blondish wig shaped into a chignon at the back of my neck and sensible black high heels. My face was covered with thick make-up -- expertly applied by my daughter a few hours earlier -- and set off by gigantic eyeglasses and a set of false teeth that fit on top of my own. Even I had to admit that I was a convincing double for the actor Robin Williams in his role as "Mrs. Doubtfire."

As I stood waiting, I turned to look at the sidewalk I had just traversed. I was tempted to run back down it and call Fred later to tell him I'd had a last-minute emergency.

Too late. The door flew open.

Fred stood before me, in a flowing black Dracula cape,

blood dripping from the edges of his mouth where presumably his fangs had pierced his lip.

In other words, he looked just the way he always did.

He looked at me blankly.

Am I supposed to say "trick or treat," I wondered.

"Yes...?" he said.

I decided to have some fun with him. I put on a fake falsetto voice with a British accent and squeaked, "Is this where the birthday boy lives?" The sound of my own voice almost made me laugh.

"Uh, yes..." he said. "But you've got me fooled -- I have no idea who you are!"

"Really, puppet?" I said. "Well, I certainly know who you are!"

He looked skeptical -- and greatly intrigued -- so he opened the door and said, "Yes...well, come in..."

I could tell he was frantically going through his guest list in his head to see if he could identify me.

The party was filled mostly with people I didn't know, although there were three or four members of Fred's staff, plus his wife, all of whom I knew very well. None of them recognized me either, and Fred was soon trotting me around from one group to the next, asking, "Can any of you tell me who this is?" I smiled sweetly and played along in my fake British accent, but my teeth were beginning to grind on my gums and the whole party on my nerves. Finally I'd had enough. I popped my teeth out and said, "Fred! It's me: Rex!"

From the look on his face I could see that he was having a hard time grasping that it was me. Did he think Mrs. Doubtfire had dropped by to wish him a happy birthday and was now putting on a Rex costume just to mess with him? I couldn't tell and, frankly, at that point I didn't care. I just wanted to unstuff my bra and kick back with a martini.

But I did win "best costume" that night -- and I didn't even have to wear a sombrero.

Thank-You Notes

I received a thank-you note from a baby the other day. This is a bright, attractive child; but, just for the record, I've never bought into that "all babies are cute" stuff, because I've seen babies who are so ugly they made me jump the first time I laid eyes on them.

But not this baby. This baby really is cute -- and intelligent, apparently. She has, at less than six months, learned how to form beautiful cursive letters into grammatically correct and accurately spelled sentences.

In other words, this six-month-old knows how to do things many adults don't.

Her signature is a little sketchy, however. It looks like it might have been done in crayon by the family cat.

My hunch is that even though the note came on a smart little card printed with the baby's full name, her mother probably stole one of those cards and wrote the note herself -- and then tried to make me think the kid did it by coyly using a crayon for the signature.

Hey, I don't care. I was just shocked to get a written thank-you note.

The whole thank-you note thing has become as important as world peace and the next winner of "American Idol." People fight about it all the time. If you read *Ask Amy,* as I do, you know that the subject of thank-you notes comes up from time to time. The letters seem to fall into two categories: either thoughtful, generous people who are surrounded by greedy, self-absorbed ingrates or the terminally lazy who feel entitled to get gifts without acknowledging them.

As you can tell, I have no strong opinion on this subject.

I write thank-you notes. I hate writing them, but I do. Lately, I've taken to writing "please, no gifts" on invitations simply because it's easier. If people don't give me anything, I don't have to thank them for it.

Our friends and neighbors, Helen and Geoff, have gone one better. We now have a standing rule between the four of us: no thank-you notes. It wasn't always so. For years, when we ate at their house, which was about three times a week, we would send a thank-you note the next day. But there were many meals, and I'm not that clever, so I quickly ran out of ways to say how much we had enjoyed our evening with them.

I knew I had to do something, so on one of the rare occasions they came to our house, instead of us going to theirs (they're funny that way; they seem to prefer eating dinner at their house -- where the food is actually edible), I caught Helen as they were leaving and said, "You are our best friends. You do so much for us. Do you think we are close enough to dispense with some of the formalities of our friendship?"

She looked at me suspiciously. She knows me, and knew I was up to something.

"Such as...?" she said.

"Well, I've been thinking. We've just had a nice dinner together -- sorry again about the burnt pasta -- and I know you will go home and write us a thank-you note, because you always do. Do you suppose we know each other well enough to skip it this time? It would be a great relief to us. ..."

She thought about it and, probably because she was wondering how in the world she could find any polite way of describing the meal they'd just consumed, she said, "Okay, but only on one condition: that you stop sending us thank-you notes, too."

"You got it," I said, barely containing my glee. I'm the one who was always writing the thank-you notes -- all she had to do was shop and pay for the groceries, do the chopping and baking and cooking and cleaning up. Finally, I was off the hook. Now all we would need to do is show up and eat. What friends!

Other people don't get off as easily. I figure if I spend fifty or a hundred bucks on a gift, I deserve some sort of written acknowledgement. My own kids, who are perfect in every way and have no faults whatsoever, are fanatical about sending written thank-you notes for every gift they receive -- even gifts from me. And no, it's not because I threaten to disinherit them if they don't. I don't have to. They figured that out on their own.

A few years ago we were bicycling in the south of France, and by "we," I mean Brad. I drove a rental car on the same route, so I did my share of pedaling -- it's just that my pedal was an accelerator.

We were part of an organized group. Each day the cyclists would bicycle to the next town on our itinerary, while the tour operator schlepped the bags in his van. I was the only person with a rental car.

One day we stayed in the town of Vence, which is on the Riviera inland from Nice. A nice couple on the same trip asked at breakfast one morning if we would be going into Nice during our layover. We hadn't planned to, so I asked why they wanted to know. "Well, we've never seen the Mediterranean and this is the closest we'll ever come, so we thought if you were going we might ask if we could hitch a ride."

"Sure, let's do it," we said, and the four of us took off for a very pleasant visit to the beach in which our friends were able to dip their toes in the Mediterranean and I was able to sit down on the sand. The only problem with sitting on the sand in Nice is that each grain of "sand" is about the size of a human head. We're talking rocks -- big rocks -- and very uncomfortable to walk across, much less sit on. But in France that doesn't stop people from topless sunbathing -- although I can't imagine how uncomfortable it must be to lie flat on your towel with all those boulders sticking up in the air.

We returned to our hotel in Vence for dinner that night. When we entered the dining room our friends were already there. The wife, Judy, was wearing an attractive sleeveless dress and there, on her upper arm, was what appeared to be a tattoo reading "I (heart) Rex & Brad."

Now, that's what I call a proper thank-you.

Pigeon Tales

My daughter, Elisabeth, and I flew to London one New Year's Eve so she could surprise her boyfriend Bill, who is now her husband (also known as "my son-in-law, the doctor.")

Bill's college band had been invited by the Lord Mayor of London to march in the New Year's Day parade, and Elisabeth thought it would be fun to show up unexpectedly. I always welcome an opportunity to spend extra time with my kids, so I jumped at the chance to accompany her. (And by "accompany," I mean "pay.")

When we arrived on New Year's Eve day, we checked into our hotel, which was nowhere near Bill's, and set out on foot to explore the city. We would eventually end up at his hotel where she planned to jump out from behind a pillar and shout "Boo!"

En route, we found ourselves in front of Buckingham Palace at the memorial to Queen Victoria. As we stood in awe of the lovely marble statue of the queen herself, a pigeon landed on her head and left his own statement of opinion about the old gal.

"How rude!" my daughter said.

"Obviously not a royalist," I observed.

The pigeon, looking at us as though he were listening intently, made another deposit as if to underscore the point.

"Well, Honey," I said. "That's a bit like life, isn't it? Some days you're the pigeon and some days you're the statue."

"That's not original, Dad," she said. I was only half-listening to her, and had stopped talking because I noticed there were pigeons all around us -- milling about our feet, flying back and forth between various points on the statue. It looked like they were getting ready to attack.

"Let's get out of here," I said. "I hate pigeons. They're nothing but rats with wings."

We continued our trek to find Bill, which we eventually did, and Elisabeth actually did surprise him. I gave them some time to themselves before we agreed to meet for dinner later, and I made my way back to our hotel.

I got lost, but I didn't care. Part of the fun of travel, for me, is getting lost. I do not travel to jungles or cities with a crime rate higher than, say, Holcomb, Kansas, where the worst thing that ever happened was the murder of the Clutter family, as immortalized by Truman Capote.

Okay, so maybe that's not the best example.

As I walked back, I noticed that several pigeons seemed to be following me. I thought back to my conversation with Elisabeth and wondered if I'd said something that might have offended them. I decided it must have been that crack about rats with wings. I hastened my step.

I really don't like pigeons, and while I'm sure we have plenty of them in the United States (I seem to recall one or two in New York City), they are ubiquitous in Europe.

In France, people actually eat them.

Brad celebrated a milestone birthday on one of our recent trips to France, and I believe the timing of the trip was to ensure that I couldn't do a big blow-out for him at home, with all his friends and family attending.   He doesn't like a lot of fanfare.

Since it would be just the two of us, I scouted around ahead of time to find a Michelin-rated restaurant for his birthday dinner.   I found a place that had gotten a rave review in the *New York Times*, so I made a reservation months in advance.

The day before his birthday we hiked up to the place to check it out.   There wasn't much to see since it was during the day and the street gates were closed, but as with most French restaurants, the menu board was posted outside. My French is rudimentary -- and that's stretching it -- but I can usually make my way through a menu.   But when I got to the word "pigeon," I thought I'd discovered a French word I'd never seen or heard before.   I said, "Brad, what's "pid-g-ee-on"?" -- pronouncing it as I thought Maurice Chevalier or Carla Bruni Sarkozy might.

"It's pigeon.   You know, the fat gray birds that poop on statues," he said.

"What?" I said incredulously.   "You mean they serve those filthy things as food in this fancy restaurant?"

"Apparently."

Well, I was beside myself.   I decided that wouldn't be my choice for dinner the next night, and when I saw the price, it was further confirmation.   It was forty-eight euros -- about sixty U.S. dollars at the time.   When I questioned this, Brad said, "Well, the menu mentions aromatic herbs and dried fruits..."

"Ha!   In other words, some fat pigeon was flying around and ate some herbs and fruit out of the garbage and this restaurant just popped him in the oven for dinner. No, thank you. If I wanted to eat a pigeon, I'd stab a fork through one on our window ledge."

The next night I ordered fish.

A few days later, I had another pigeon encounter. We had rented an apartment in Aix-en-Provence, a charming town in the south of France. Brad had a French lesson every morning and I used the time to explore the town and shop.   One day I happened to run into one of his classmates, an attractive young woman named Holly from Bozeman, Montana. As I approached her, I noticed she was seated at the edge of a busy street on the curb, next to a pigeon, eating her lunch. (I mean Holly was eating her own lunch, not the pigeon's.) I stopped and we chatted a few minutes, and she talked of her concern about an upcoming trip to Paris, since the authorities had just issued an elevated terror alert for Americans traveling in Europe.

I tried to reassure her, telling her I was certain that was just a precautionary thing and I wouldn't give it too much thought, but as I was talking I noticed the pigeon eyeing her sandwich.   I told her I thought she had more important things to worry about.

Now that I'm writing about pigeons, I recall yet another story that occurred just a few months earlier, when we were in Nice. We had stopped at a cafe called Fenocchio in the Place Rossetti, located in a square in front of the Cathedral Sainte-Reparate.

Just as we were seated there was an enormous explosion

-- like a bomb going off. I was in the process of climbing under the table, as we were taught to do during bomb scares in third grade (atomic bombs, that is -- the kind that can't penetrate third-grade desks) when Brad suggested that it might have been a cannon, designed to scare off the pigeons.

"A cannon?" I asked incredulously. "You mean they make that kind of noise just to scare the pigeons?"

About this time the waiter appeared with our coffees and I noticed his hands were trembling slightly. After he'd left, I said, "You may be right. Our waiter's nerves are frazzled -- and whose wouldn't be if they had to listen to that all day."

As if to prove my point, the cannon went off again. While I was mopping up my spilled coffee I noticed a pigeon on a ledge less than three feet from our table who seemed to be showing an inordinate interest in my croissant.

"Oh, I think it will eventually drive them away," Brad said.

I happened to be looking at the pigeon as Brad delivered that line and I swear the pigeon, overhearing him, actually rolled his beady little eyes as if to say, "You gotta be kidding."

A bit later the church bells began ringing -- it was noon -- but they didn't ring just twelve times, they rang about a hundred times as though the bell ringer was on crack. I looked at the pigeon again -- he hadn't budged -- and he rolled his eyes again as if to say, "I know. I have to listen to all this all day long."

For some reason, my mind flashed back to that day in London as Elisabeth and I stood in front of the statue of

Queen Victoria. As if on cue, the pigeon on the ledge above us edged closer to where we were seated, just below. I could tell what he was getting ready to do, so I executed a herky-jerky movement involving my hands, arms and legs which was designed to frighten him away, which it did -- with the added effect of startling the entire table of tourists seated next to us.

I had decided this wasn't going to be my day to be the statue.

Pack Out My What?

Some people are outdoorsy, some are not.

Brad, for example, has climbed most of Colorado's Fourteeners. A fourteener is one of 53 peaks measuring more than 14,000 feet in elevation. I will climb them when they install escalators.

I had dropped him off at the trailhead for a three-day backpack on Snowmass Mountain, just outside of Aspen, and while he was unloading his gear from the car, I spotted a sign across the parking lot and went over to see what it said.

Please pack out your poop.

I studied it carefully to see if it had been defaced. Surely it was supposed to say something else. I looked around for a hidden camera -- to see if somebody was waiting to see my reaction. I was about to give them one.

"Please pack out your poop," I read again.

Excuse me?

I asked Brad about it. "Why does it say that?" I asked.

He looked at me like I was a slow child.

"Good campers pack out their poop because they don't

want to negatively impact the environment."

That's all I needed to know. I don't want to hurt the environment, so I should obviously spend more time indoors. I will schlep a lot of stuff: electronics, my own luggage, groceries, and children two and under. But I am not carrying my poop around.

This is yet another reason why I am a hotel person, and the more stars the better. I am very suspicious of people who say they prefer camping out to staying in a four-star hotel.

I believe we dishonor the sacrifices made by our pioneering forefathers and mothers if we choose to stay outdoors when a hotel is readily available.

Imagine what it was like for those early adventurers. They were seeking nothing more than a better life for themselves -- one that included air-conditioning, down pillows, and room service, for starters.

And who wouldn't want those things? It's easy for me to conjure up a picture of some guy driving an ox-cart across the dry, dusty fields of the flat states, the back of the wagon filled with his wife and half a dozen snot-nosed kids with all their earthly belongings (spinning wheel, shovel, butter churn, etc.) At night, they didn't have the option of pulling under a porte cochère and letting the valet park their wagon for a mere twenty-five dollars a night -- but if they had, I'll bet they would have done it in a heartbeat (complaining about the fee the whole time, just like we do today.)

No, they pulled into a circle with the other wagons and built a big fire in the middle to keep them warm and safe from danger, which lurked all around them, including snakes and other forms of nature. Snakes is all I need to think about when I conjure up this scenario. When I think of snakes, I change the channel.

Our foremothers and fathers didn't even have the basic necessities such as a goose down, waterproof sleeping bag like you can get these days at REI for a mere seven hundred dollars. Rather, they slept on the ground, on an old blanket which was probably crawling with the same insects that crawled around in their hair.

Do you think they would have declined the offer of a big comfortable bed made with clean, luxurious linens? Or a shiny Carrera marble bathroom with porcelain tub, gleaming stainless-steel fixtures, and Kiehl's toiletries? How about big, white, absorbent, 100% Egyptian cotton towels?

Not on your life they wouldn't.

Nor will I, in honor of their memory.

That's not to say I stay only in luxurious, top-of-the line hotels. Like most people, I've stayed in my share of flea-bags -- but never as my first choice. The last hotel we stayed in was on a driving trip between California and Colorado. We were assigned to a room on the bottom floor, but at least we could keep our eye on the parking lot and listen to the kids in the room above us practice their jumping. In times like this I still remind myself of what the pioneers put up with, so I try not to complain too much. Besides, I stupidly left my new sneakers in the room when we left -- and a hotel employee actually found them and mailed them back to me. Trust me when I say that never happened to the pioneers.

As you may have guessed, I take a special interest in the room amenities at a hotel -- and I am happy to report that these days, hotels are going to great lengths to make sure their rooms are stocked with every creature comfort.

High on my list of most desirable amenities is the in-room safe. Many hotels have them these days, and they provide an excellent place to store your valuables -- assuming your valuables can fit into a container the size of a toaster oven so it can be carried out of the hotel hidden under a maid's skirt.

When we stay in a hotel that lacks an in-room safe, we simply hide our valuables in the room, in places nobody would ever think to look -- including us. This is an interesting game, because inevitably we forget where we've put something, which requires asking the maid if she happened to find, say, our passports -- upon which she marches right over to the bedside table, removes the drawer and shows us where they are "hidden."

For obvious reasons, we always use the same easy-to-remember lock combination -- my birthday -- because, according to the warnings printed on the safe, if you forget the combination you're up you-know-what creek without a paddle. In those situations, the hotel arranges for a professional locksmith to come out and drill the safe open -- which costs considerably more than a new paddle for the aforementioned creek.

But even that, as it turns out, isn't always true.

We were in an upscale hotel in Europe not long ago where we made use of the safe every time we left the room. We put our passports, wallets, extra cash, cell phones and even my laptop computer in it, entered our usual combination, and walked out.

One afternoon when we returned from the pool, I dutifully entered the combination and...zip. Nothing happened. I looked closely at the electronic readout and it said, in robotic letters, "ERROR." I pushed "cancel," waited a minute, and tried again.

This time the printout said, "ERROR-2."

Oh, so you're keeping track, eh?

This was a panicky situation if ever there was one, and I suddenly flashed on an image of some inept locksmith with a blowtorch opening the door while simultaneously incinerating everything inside it.

I realized I'd better have a witness for the third try so I wouldn't be accused of foolishly entering the wrong number. As it turned out, the potential witness and potential accuser were the same person, who was sitting two feet away on the edge of the bed.

"Oh, Brad...?" I said, trying to act nonchalant. "The safe doesn't seem to be working."

"Are you sure you got it right?" he asked, obviously forgetting that (a) it is the same in every hotel we stay in; and (b) it is my birthday.

"Well, yes, actually. If you're asking if I know my own birthday, then yes, I think I do."

"No, I mean are you sure you pressed the buttons correctly?"

This stumped me for a second. *Gosh...do I know how to push buttons? When was the last time I pushed one? Did I do it right? Isn't it merely a matter of extending one's finger and exerting pressure? What have I been doing all these years?*

I kept these thoughts to myself, though, and responded witheringly, "Yes, well, why don't you watch me do it to see that I do it correctly."

And he did. I re-entered the numbers slowly and carefully, making sure he watched me carefully the entire time.

ERROR-3!   It might as well have added, AND YOU'RE OUT! -- because, indeed, we were.   Pushing even one button thereafter resulted in a terrible beeping sound that could be heard almost two feet away, thereby alerting absolutely nobody.   ERROR-3 continued to flash on the little readout.

At this point I had pretty much resigned myself to leaving our cell phones, passports, car keys, wallets and all our money in the safe forever until I remembered that my computer was also inside.   This made it a real emergency.   We had to have help now!

As luck would have it, I opened the room door to go to the front desk and explain my predicament and practically walked right into the arms of the doorman -- who, I happened to remember, spoke perfect English.   I resisted the impulse to ask him why he was wandering the halls rather than manning the door.

Instead, I outlined the situation and said, "Do you know what the procedure is to get this fixed?"

He smile broadly and said, "But of course!"   Then he reached into his pocket, pulled out a key, and walked into our room and unlocked the safe.   Problem solved!   By the doorman!   The doorman who apparently has a key to all the room safes!   I can't express how comforting this was.

In retrospect, I think we might have been better off hiding our valuables in the mini-bar which seems to be checked at least four times a day to see if anybody's been stupid enough to consume a fifteen-euro Toblerone bar.

This set me to wondering: where did our forefathers keep their valuables?   I'm pretty sure they didn't have safes in the back of those covered wagons, and even if they did, I'm positive they wouldn't have been able to find a doorman — since they didn't even have doors.

And that is why they came west: to find a luxury hotel with top-of-the-line toiletries -- and safes. And doors.

Should we do less than honor their memory by taking advantage of these wonderful conveniences? One can only imagine what they would have done with a fifteen-euro Toblerone bar.

No Translation Needed

The only time I cheated in school was during my second year of college when I was caught looking up the answers to a quiz in French class.

My professor, a pasty-faced Francophile from some place in Ohio, went by the name "Monsieur Patz" -- which he insisted was pronounced "potts" but should have been pronounced "putz" because that's what he was.

And yes, that was his real name.

When he realized I had been looking up the answers to his quiz, he had every right to give me a failing grade or kick me out of his class. Either punishment would have been preferable to what he actually did.

He stormed over to my desk and barked something in French, which I couldn't understand (since I couldn't look it up) before he noticed the blank look on my face and resorted to English.

He ordered me to the front of the classroom, where he proceeded to pull down a rolled-up map (of France, coincidentally) until the cord could be wrapped around my neck, which is what he did with it. He then made me stand there until class ended, as though I were being publicly hanged until dead.

I suppose it's an understatement to say I didn't like him.

I've taken other language classes since then (German, Spanish, more French), but I seem to lack the "language gene." Brad, on the other hand, could easily learn any of those languages and a hundred others with about fifteen minutes of instruction.

Note that I said he *could*. That doesn't mean he will -- and even when he does learn another language, he never lets on that he knows it. In France, for example, one would expect him to do all the talking since he speaks French fluently. But he doesn't. Rather, he allows me to make a fool of myself -- a look of detached amusement on his face -- as I try to ask directions, order dinner, or purchase a cup of coffee. He claims he is merely "acting French" -- and therefore "on strike."

"Well, I'm going to go 'on strike' in a moment," I say. "So you'd better start running."

Then, when I least expect it, he will strike up a French conversation that for some reason involves a lot of sympathetic nodding towards me.

This happened when we went to get haircuts one day. The barbershop we found had only one person in it: the barber. When we walked in, Brad acted like he didn't know why we were there, so I had to open with my standard line, "Parlez-vous anglais?" *Do you speak English?*

"Non," came the reply.

"Ah," I said, turning to Brad who was already flipping through magazines like he was in the Christian Science Reading Room. "Excuse me, Brad...will you please tell this man we would like to get haircuts?" I was talking through gritted teeth with my eyes bugged out like I was about to have a stroke.

He finally spoke a sentence or two in French which caused the man to develop a concerned look on his face and guide me toward the barber chair as though he were dealing with an elderly person or an imbecile.

I sat down.

I can't sit still for long without talking, whether I know the language or not, so knowing the barber couldn't understand a word I was saying, I simply said every nonsensical thing that entered my head.

"I was hoping that you might shave my head bald, Monsieur...and then paint a big target on it. Or you could just slit my throat while you pretend to shave me..."

"Oui, oui, Monsieur," he said.

"And then, when it is my friend's turn, I'd like you to dye his hair green, please."

"Oui, Monsieur. Oui." he replied.

Brad, who had been listening, was not amused and finally put down his magazine. He came to my side where he addressed the barber in French. At this point the barber became quite animated, and the two of them talked across me as if they were neighbors talking across the fence.

After he finished my haircut and Brad got his, we were walking down the street and I said, "What was that long conversation with the barber all about?"

"Oh, I just told him you were a mental patient and had gotten hold of the scissors and cut your own hair. I asked him to tidy it up a bit before I had to take you back to the mental hospital."

Ho ho.

Sometimes I don't understand French people even when they are speaking English. On the same trip there was a knock on our door one day and, when I opened it, our landlord greeted me by saying, "Have you seen a naked man?"

This created an immediate problem because I wasn't quite sure what he meant. Since I've been in a few locker rooms during my lifetime, obviously I've seen a naked man. I even recall seeing Brad in his birthday suit a time or two. So, somehow I doubted that he was really asking if I'd *ever* seen a naked man.

Then I thought, maybe he's asking if I've seen a naked man because he's lost one -- the way you might ask someone if they saw a tall man with purple hair run by with your purse.

But that didn't make sense either, since we were on the third floor and wouldn't have seen anybody run by -- naked or otherwise.

Finally, I gave up. I couldn't figure out what he was asking, so I said, in French, "Je suis désolé mais je ne comprends pas." *I'm sorry, but I don't understand.*

He said, in English, "You know...last night...across the street...the man was parading naked in front of his window all night?" By this time Brad had come to the door to join me. I repeated what the landlord had just said, and Brad confirmed, in French, that no, we hadn't seen such a thing, but thanks for asking.

After he left, we looked at each other and then raced to the window to start our surveillance. Unfortunately, he never materialized again -- even though we spent the next two months glued to the window.

It was unusual that our landlord would even try out his

English on us, because typically the French are reluctant to speak English with Americans because they worry that they'll "get it wrong." (Unlike Americans who don't hesitate for a minute to butcher the French language because they don't care if it's wrong or not.)

The greatest compliment you can pay a French person is to tell them their English is good -- so that's what I do every chance I get. The reaction is always the same: they beam, then they act embarrassed, then they deny it. "Oh non, Monsieur...my English...eet ees not so good...it is...how you say...'orrible...."

But, because you've made the effort, they will make more of an effort not to overcharge you.

My technique doesn't always work, though. One day at the market I overheard a man speaking English, so I sidled up to him and said, "Monsieur, I must tell you -- your English is quite good!"

He gave me a withering look and said, "I should hope so. I'm from Chicago." After that I tried to listen a little longer before I used that line.

But then I came up with an even better one.

Since Brad was in class every morning, I sometimes found myself wanting to interact with someone -- anyone -- who spoke English. Again I found myself at the market, this time to shop for dinner. My list consisted of chicken, jam and cough drops, but only the chicken would be used for dinner (the chicken appeared to be in perfect health, other than being dead, so the cough drops were for me.)

While standing in line to pay, I heard the woman in front of me speaking English so, being a smart aleck, I said, "That doesn't sound like French to me!" (Later I would learn not to use that particular line on French people, since they don't appreciate it.) But since this woman was clearly American, so she laughed. We chatted together as we walked out of the store and before long I realized we had walked at least two blocks together.

I learned she was married to a physician and that they were from San Francisco but had been living in France for ten years. We continued to walk, blathering away in English, when I became concerned that I was taking too much of her time.

"Oh my gosh," I said. "Listen to me. I've taken so much of your time you'll think I'm a Mormon trying to convert you!"

She laughed uproariously, because guess what religion she was. Then she added, "Actually, I was just getting ready to do that to you."

It was my turn to laugh and point out the obvious (at least from my point of view): "Oh thanks, but I don't think I'd fit in."

Somehow I don't think she had yet picked up on the fact that she was talking so a gay man, so she insisted that of *course* I would fit in -- and asked if I would be interested in coming to dinner sometime. I thanked her and said, "Sure, I'll ask my partner, *Brad,* (emphasizing the maleness of "Brad") and we'll let you know when you call."

She didn't call, and I never saw her again, so we didn't get together for dinner. But I wish we had. I liked her. (And, being from California, her English was quite good.)

My most terrifying language moment came during the same trip when, once again, I was in the grocery store. (It sounds like I did nothing but shop, which is almost true since the refrigerator in our apartment was originally made for Barbie's Dream House.)

On this particular trip I had to buy some clear plastic wrap -- we use Saran Wrap at home -- and after moving slowly along every aisle in the store looking for it, I finally gave up and asked an employee who was mopping the floor if he knew where it was kept.

He didn't speak a word of English, so I had to act it out. (Note: if you ever get "Saran Wrap" as your clue in Pictionary or Charades, take another card.) I was holding a shopping list in my hand -- written on paper -- so I held it up and pointed to it while saying loudly, "Paper! Paper!" And then I held it right in front of my eyes and said, "Clear! See through!" moving it quickly to the side with each word to illustrate that I couldn't see through it when it was in front of my eyes, but I could when I moved it, which anybody could tell meant "see-through."

Well, it made perfect sense to me.

Weary of the conversation, he finally latched on to the concept of paper ("Oui! Pay-pare" he tried to say in English) and walked me over to the shelves which held toilet paper and pointed dramatically. He seemed so proud of himself for figuring out what I wanted that I felt obligated to buy a roll as a gesture of thanks.

But it wasn't very effective for wrapping food to be stored in the refrigerator.

After the man went back to his mopping, I commenced a two-month search for plastic wrap. I never found any -- and, believe me, I looked in every store in town -- so I guess the French simply don't use it.

It's true that I spent a lot of time shopping in France -- mostly in grocery stores or open-air markets. The nice thing about the grocery store, as opposed to the market, is that the store has cash registers which show the total of your purchase. That means I don't have to determine if they've just asked me for "trois euros" (three) or "trois cents" (three hundred.) Making purchases at the open-air market can make a big difference in the grocery budget. When they announce what I owe them, I simply hold out a handful of money and let them take what they want. But in the grocery store, I can see the number on the cash register which enables me to take an irritating amount of time to shuffle through my bills and coins before finally handing over the correct amount.

One day, I was waiting at the end of a line of four people, holding toilet paper and a few other items, when the clerk shouted back at me, "Blah, blah, blah, blah!" That isn't verbatim, but it was in French, so I don't actually know what it was.

I quickly adopted the look of a person who is visually and hearing impaired -- staring into space as though I didn't see or hear what she was saying. At this, the four people in front of me quickly turned around to see why I hadn't responded.

The woman standing directly in front of me took one look at me -- I hadn't said a word -- and said in French-accented English, "You're an American, aren't you?"

I checked to see if I was wearing red, white and blue, but then I realized she was doing what all French people do when they see someone acting stupid: they assume (correctly, as it often turns out) that they are American.

"Um, yes, I am," I said.

"Ah!" she said. "The cashier is telling you that you are to be her last customer, and she asks that you inform anyone else who comes to join the line that it is now closed."

Oh sure, I thought. That ought to be easy -- provided everyone just waits here for a few minutes while I run out to learn how to speak French.

But it turned out okay. All of a sudden I remembered the French word for closed -- "fermé" -- which I politely said to each of the next ten or twelve people who came running up to join the line. They all seemed to understand, too. Each one of them said, without exception, "D'accord, merci."

Okay. Thank you.

No translation needed.

Wake Up and Smell the Bacon in the Street

Until I met Brad, I thought Corsica was a Chevrolet model from the 60s. I didn't know it was a French island -- even though I'd been to France dozens of times by then.

In my defense, there are a lot of people who don't know it is a *French* island, including a whole bunch of Italians who still think it belongs to them.

This, understandably, causes some friction.

I may hear from the tourist bureau about this, but Corsica isn't my favorite place. There are several reasons for this, not the least of which is that some people maintain the island is controlled by the Mafia.

I'm just sayin'...

A few years ago Brad signed up for a cycling trip on Corsica, and I went along to keep him company. It was to be a two-week trip with about 500 miles of cycling -- a curious itinerary, since the entire island is only 114 miles long and 52 miles wide. We would soon discover that a lot of back and forth was involved.

The trip included some 47,000 feet of climbing which, for the uninitiated, means the cyclists pedal that far uphill.

Yes, up.

I drove the same route in a rental car. I was exhausted.

Our journey started on the mainland, in Nice, where we arrived a couple of days early to acclimate to European time and eggs. I confirmed, once again, that the scrambled eggs they serve in France -- anywhere in France -- are unlike any we get at home. This would be okay if the difference was, say, that they were sprinkled with caviar, or included onions or chives, but that's not the difference. The difference is, they're powdered. And vile. And I don't like them.

So, I make-do by eating chocolate croissants.

We spent our time in Nice exploring on foot, since we weren't renting a car until we landed on Corsica. Each day we took a long walk and saw how nice Nice really is.

One morning we found ourselves down at the marina where there were at least a dozen enormous yachts anchored. One in particular -- a huge, shiny, sleek black thing that looked more like an airplane than a yacht -- seemed to be just waiting for us jump on and go for a sail.

I said to Brad, "Do you suppose we could get a yacht like this someday?"

"No," he said, without hesitation. "But maybe we can get that one over there.…" He pointed at a little dinghy floating in the corner of the marina.

Har-har.

From there we needed some lunch, and I spotted a little restaurant called "Le Joke Café." I wanted to go in, but Brad refused. He thought the food might taste funny.

It took me at least half an hour to realize he'd made a joke.

The next day we took a cab down to the harbor to

board the boat which would take us to Corsica -- roughly an eight-hour trip. Brad had told me in advance that "Corsica Ferries" would be taking us to the island, but I didn't realize until we got to the pier that he meant a ferry boat and not a couple of gay guys with a yacht.

Double har-har.

I will admit that Corsica is scenic. It is the most mountainous island in the Mediterranean and has over 200 beaches. It also has more hogs than you can shake a stick at, and believe me, you will.

Early in the trip the group cycled from the town of Porticcio, on the sea, to the town of Corte, which is right in the middle of the island. I hung around the hotel for a while to give the cyclists a chance to get well on their way. By driving behind them, I will eventually catch-up and be in a position to help if needed.

As I began following the route, I was astonished to see how narrow some of the roads were. In many places, the road was only wide enough for two fat pigs -- assuming they are walking single file. Doing a U-turn on these roads simply isn't possible. It would be like turning your car around on a sidewalk. First you say, "Why is this road no wider than a sidewalk?" Then you say, "What am I doing on this sidewalk, anyway?"

This happened to me numerous times, and each time I had to continue to the next town where there was usually a roundabout, which I used to aim the car in the right direction.

Even worse was when I encountered another driver coming from the opposite direction. That presented a moral dilemma: do I simply drive off the edge of the mountain, plunging thousands of feet to my death, or do I try to push them off? Thankfully, each time the other driver gave in and backed down to a place where I could pass.

Sometimes it wasn't another driver I had to worry about, it was an animal. This is when I had to wonder if I had somehow missed the sign telling me I was in a game preserve.

The feral pigs were the worst. They were everywhere -- and most of them were about the size of a Smart Car. That would be fine if it meant we got bacon with breakfast ("Monsieur, your powdered eggs and bacon are ready."), but we never did. After a while I began fantasizing about crashing into a pig just so I could get some bacon.

But pigs weren't the only problem. Around one corner I came upon a bull standing in the middle of the road, snorting -- just like in a cartoon. He gave me a look, but I stared him down -- as I went sailing by at 65 miles per hour.

Half an hour later I came upon a hundred sheep being herded down the road like passengers through airport security. I had no choice but to stop and take in the smell of wet wool as it paraded past my car. I had my window down until the smell registered and I put it up just as one of the sheep looked like it was going to jump into the car with me.

Shortly after that encounter, I came around a corner to find three men in camouflage clothing walking out of the woods. Since they were carrying guns, I thought I should tell them that the sheep went "that-a-way," but then I realized people don't hunt sheep with guns. Looking a bit more closely, I saw that they looked like they'd just stepped out of the movie "Deliverance." I stepped on it to keep from becoming their next victim.

Around the next bend I came upon a little town which had a gas station, complete with an attendant who stood with his hand on the gas pump and a lighted cigarette dangling from his lips. I decided I could wait to get gas -- preferring a station that wasn't likely to explode while I was there. As I watched in my rearview mirror, I could actually envision the place going up in flames. "Barbecued pork, coming right up!" I brightened when I realized at least I'd get some bacon.

I finally reached the hotel by mid-afternoon, well ahead of the cyclists whom I had passed at various intervals along the way (usually being chased by pigs, bulls, or sheep.)

I approached the front desk with some apprehension, as I knew I was in a remote part of France and it was unlikely that anybody would speak English. I was right, but the proprietress greeted me warmly and even though she spoke only French, she had the good sense to offer me a *bière* -- which tasted especially good after my several encounters with death.

I did notice, however, that the beer -- a local brew called "Pietra" -- seemed to have sand at the bottom of the bottle. Brad told me later that it was chestnut beer and that what I had seen was chestnut residue.

Okay...nuts in my beer. No matter -- I drank it anyway.

After I finished it, I asked the proprietress if the hotel had wifi or, as they pronounce it in France, "wee-fee." Asking that question is so simple and straightforward, even I could do it.

"Excusez-moi, Madame. Avez-vous 'wee-fee'?"

She looked at me blankly.

"You know," I said, trying to think of a way to act out what a computer connection might look like to someone who lived where pigs roam freely. "Com-pute-err?" "Co-nex-ee-ohn?"

Still nothing...but I could tell she really wanted to get this one, and she was listening and watching intently.

To act it out, I put my hands on the counter in front of me and acted like I was typing on a keyboard. "You know...com-pute-err?" I said again.

"Ah!" she said, smiling broadly. "Com-pute-ehr! Oui, oui! Com-pute-ehr!"

But now I had to communicate what I wanted to do with the *com-pute-ehr*. "Con-ex-see-ohn?" I asked.

This she understood immediately. "Voila! Oui! Con-ex-ee-ohn!" She pushed a pad of paper and pen toward me so I could write down what she was about to tell me and walked over to the cash register. Lifting it into the air like a weight lifter, she began reading to me: "Numéro...un...deux...trois...." followed by another sixteen or so numbers. I dutifully wrote each one down. When she had finished, I realized I was now in possession of the serial number of the cash register. What she expected me to do with this, I have no idea, but I thanked her profusely and requested another *bière*.

Our next hotel wasn't quite as friendly. There was some speculation among members of the group that it was owned by Germans, since it was somewhat spartan.

Amazingly, their guess was spot-on.

It was hot and humid when we arrived, so as soon as I got to my room, I began looking for the air-conditioner. I found it high up on the wall where nobody could possibly reach it. Since its vents seemed to point toward the ceiling, all I needed to do was defy gravity so I could lie down on the ceiling, and I'd be all set.

But first I would need to find the thermostat. As it turns out, there wasn't one -- or even a wall switch to flip on and off. I concluded it must be operated remotely, like a television, so I began searching for a remote control. I looked everywhere: under the bed, between the mattresses and even inside the toilet tank, in case some previous disgruntled occupant had thrown it there just for meanness. It wasn't there.

Finally, frustrated, I went down to the front desk to ask for help. I had previously nicknamed the clerk "Frau Faghetaboudit" because she looked and acted like a guard at a women's prison. She informed me, in clipped English with a decidedly German accent, that one must "check out" the remote control as one would a library book.

I did so and soon stood below what I hoped was a soothing flow of cool air. I couldn't tell for sure, since I was still under the influence of gravity and therefore anchored to the floor. The air-conditioner, on the other hand, was blowing on the ceiling.

Like all good Germans, Frau Faghetaboudit was still in control, because at 9 o'clock that night the air conditioner abruptly stopped working, and it didn't come back on until 10 o'clock the next morning. One of the cyclists told us at breakfast that he went downstairs to complain about the outage only to be told, "You are cool enough. Go to sleep."

We all laughed at his story until, a few minutes later, we were served our "*compleat*" breakfast, which consisted only of croissants and juice. That was fine with me -- that's what I call a diet! -- but the cyclists would have preferred something a bit more substantial for the arduous day ahead. We knew better than to ask Frau Faghetaboudit, as we knew she would probably just say "You are full enough. Shut up."

Ah, the Germans. What would we do without them? Can't live with 'em, and...well, that's all.

Daily Life in France

I tell everybody I meet that I love France. When the cable guy shows up to fix our cable service (which sucks) I tell him how much I love France.

My doctor told me at my last check-up that he and his wife were planning a trip to Japan. "Oh, I can relate," I said. "I love France!"

I love all things French: French fries, French-kissing, French vanilla ice-cream, French doors, French poodles (as long as they're animatronic), French bread, French dip and French dressing. Well, on that last one, I really prefer Roquefort -- which is also French!

But that doesn't mean I'm blind to the shortcomings of France. Like all Americans, there are many things I take for granted, such as not having to show an ID card on demand (except if you are driving an automobile, or all the time in Arizona.)

I also assume that windows have screens to keep out the bugs, but this is a decidedly American invention, along with shower curtains -- not to keep out the bugs but to keep the water from flying all over the bathroom, including into the electric sockets.

When I asked about a garbage disposal when we rented an apartment in France, the landlord didn't know what I was talking about. In France, the stuff you usually put down a garbage disposal is thrown into the regular trash and placed on the street (down three flights of stairs, and then back up again.) There on the street it is picked up twice a day: an hour before you want to get up in the morning and an hour after you fall asleep at night. On this subject I don't know which is worse: the noise a garbage disposal makes (especially with a spoon in it) or the noise of a trash truck staffed by Turkish rebels rumbling down the street at 5 o'clock in the morning.

Much is made of universal signage these days. I can easily spot a stop sign in France because it is octagonal, red, and has the word "STOP" printed on it. But other French signs can be a bit more of a challenge. For example, I drove all over the south of France, where I kept seeing a road sign with what appeared to be a drawing of a turtle on it. I don't know how long it took me to figure out it was warning me of a "road bump" ahead. Maybe it was about the twentieth time I banged my head against the ceiling of the car.

My favorite sign in France is actually two signs, exactly alike, which I spotted on a public bus. They featured round-headed stick figures, each holding a cane to his/her side. They were obviously meant to identify the seats beneath them as reserved for the handicapped, but I told Brad that they were reserved for "twins with canes."

As in the U.S., France has some confusing signs -- confusing to non-French speakers, that is. For example, while walking in Aix one day, we walked past the local 7-

Eleven which really isn't a 7-Eleven at all but, rather, an "8 à Huit" -- or 8 to 8. Brad says this is an excellent example of the French work ethic: their convenience stores open an hour later than ours and close three hours earlier.

On the same walk we came across a sign pointing down what appeared to be a private street that said, "Club 3eme Age." "Hey," I said to Brad. "There's a club down this street, let's check it out."

"You won't like it," was his droll response.

"How do you know?"

"Because it's not a club. It's an old folks home."

I studied the sign. I recognized the word "club," of course. And I suppose I should have figured out the word "age" was probably something to steer clear of. But I didn't get the "3eme."

"It refers to 'Stage Three,'" he said. "The French have divided life into three 'stages.' The first stage is obviously childhood. The second is middle age, and the third -- '3eme' -- refers to old age. Thus, this sign refers to an assisted living facility."

I looked down the road and saw that it was a dead-end. Literally.

We steered clear (lest someone run out and haul us back in as escapees) and continued down the street. Eventually we came upon a cafe with a rainbow flag flying just above the door. This seemed incongruous in this particular neighborhood, but we were hungry so we stopped in for lunch.

The waiter spoke passable English, so when he brought the menus to the table, I asked, "Why the rainbow flag?"

He seemed indignant that I would ask such a stupid

question -- which should have been my first clue -- but he answered, "Because this is a gay restaurant, Monsieur!"

"Great!" I said. "I'll have the gay B.L.T., please."

Another thing I'm not crazy about in France is the whole laundry thing.

In Aix, we had our own washing machine, but in other parts of France I had to schlep our clothes down to *la laverie* to wash them.

In Calvi, on Corsica, I found an empty laundromat, but it was dirty -- so much so that when I later dropped a sock on the floor, I thought about throwing it away (it was Brad's.)

Looking around, I realized I had never seen washers and dryers like this before, so I took time to study them carefully to determine, first of all, which was the washer and which was the dryer.

Then I realized I hadn't brought enough coins, so I headed down the street to the bank to get my paper euros changed into coin euros.

That proved to be a mistake, as the bank had a sign on the door stating clearly (in French and English) "no change." Well, if the bank won't change your money, who will? Desperate, I went to the convenience store (8 à Huit) across the street and tried to find something cheap to buy so they would have to give me change in coins.

While in line to buy what I hoped was gum but may have been chewing tobacco, I noticed that a woman who came into the store after me went directly to the cashier to ask her a question. I thought, "Oh sure, Madame, you go right ahead and butt in line -- I don't have anything else to do...," but then I saw she was just getting tokens for the laundromat. I put my gum/chewing tobacco back on the shelf and returned to the laundromat with my new tokens -- only to discover that the woman who cut in line at the convenience store had already gotten there and taken all the washing machines.

I had nothing better to do, so I took out my Kindle to read until her machines finished.

When it was finally my turn, I had to figure out how the machines worked. I consulted an instruction sign on the wall which had no words (thank goodness) but, rather, a series of cartoons showing a little man taking off all his clothes and putting them into a washing machine.

Oh great, I thought. Now I have to get naked in front of this strange woman. But then I noticed that the little cartoon man also seemed to be putting a certain number of tokens into the machine, so I left my clothes on and put the tokens in.

To say that the washers are small is an understatement. Using them wouldn't be unlike taking all your dirty clothes for the week and stuffing them into the glove box of your car.

But my all-time *least* favorite sign in France was right there, on the washing machine. It said "14 Euros per load."

Based on the conversion rate in effect that day, fourteen Euros converted to $18.26 U.S. dollars! The last time I looked in the U.S., coin-operated washing machines cost about seventy-five cents.

Never mind. I'll say it again: I love France!

The Pillow Goes Under Your Head

Brad lost a tooth tonight. A big gold one. Who knew he had gold teeth? He told me just after dinner that it was loose, and I cautioned him not to wiggle it so it would last until he got home. That prompted him to reach in and yank it out, after which he showed it to me like he'd made it in art class. It was big, too -- not as big as a golf ball, even though I told him it was. If it had been as big as a golf ball, we could have sold the gold alone for over a thousand bucks. When I told him that, he deadpanned, "Oh yeah. I see a Smart Car in your future."

"A Smart Car!" I said. "Well then, let's pull out all your teeth so we can get a Lexus!"

I was horrified that he pulled his own tooth out, because I require sedation just to have my teeth cleaned. Anything beyond a routine cleaning should, in my opinion, involve two or three days in the hospital. With heavy-duty painkillers.

I hasten to clarify that I do not practice dentistry as a vocation, although I have been known to practice it as a hobby on my unwitting children.

Elisabeth likes to tell a story that supposedly happened when she was growing up. She claims she had a loose tooth, and that I insisted on tying a thread to it, which I then (allegedly) attached to a door knob. After I made sure she was across the room and the string was taut, I simply slammed the door. She says that "ripped the tooth out right out of [her] head." She has borne that particular grudge for years (who can blame her?) but when she tells the story she always leaves out the part about how she kept playing with the tooth -- wiggling it, whining about it, wiggling it some more. It got on my nerves. What else was I supposed to do?

Pulling his own teeth is just one example of Brad's self-sufficiency. Here's another: when I was out on our deck, I noticed a wasp nest high up under the eaves of the roof. To me, that means one thing: call the fire department or, at the very least, the exterminators. Not Brad. He simply went into the garage, grabbed a can of bug spray and sprayed the doo-dah out of them.

When I finished running down the street to escape what I was sure would be their wrath, I looked at the can and said, "Hey wait a minute. This is *ant* spray!"

He didn't miss a beat. He said, "So, I guess now they'll have an identity crisis."

That's what we call a "Bradism," and rarely does the day pass that I don't hear one. Another example: upon opening yet another fundraising appeal from a local charity, "I can't believe how many charities there are. I think we should start our own charity."

Me: "Oh yeah? What kind of charity?"

Brad: "I don't know. Maybe we could call it the 'Make-A-Scene Foundation.'"

Bradism.

Here's another: after hearing a waiter boast about the restaurant's use of "free-range chicken," Brad said to me, "I'd think I'll order a jelly sandwich made on free-range bread."

I thought that was hilarious, but when I told the waiter he didn't seem to think it was all that funny.

Another time we were walking in a nearby park when we encountered a group of five women who were walking abreast, one with a baby carriage and two with dogs on leashes, making it practically impossible for us to get by. After they'd passed, Brad says to me, "I encountered this same group on the sidewalk last week. They looked like they were trying to form the Star of David. Only Evel Knievel could have gotten by them."

Like everybody, Brad does have his quirks -- the strangest of which is his habit of sleeping with the pillow on *top* of his face. When I first met him, I was puzzled about this, but I didn't want to hurt his feelings by pointing out that he was doing it wrong. After all, he'd been sleeping all his life -- at least during the hours when he wasn't awake -- so one would think by now he would have learned how to operate a pillow.

"Um...," I began. "Did you read the directions that came with your pillow?"

"Directions?" he said. "What directions? What are you talking about?"

"Well," I said, trying to speak slowly and kindly, "you see, the pillow is actually supposed to go *under* your head -- you know, to give you something soft to put your head *on*."

"Oh, that," he said. "Yes, I know, but I like to block

out the sound and light. I find that it makes me sleep more soundly."

"That's because you're probably about to lose consciousness and die," I said, pointing out the obvious. "No, you're not supposed to do that. You could smother."

This was quickly escalating into a full-fledged argument -- something we never do, but I wasn't about to let it go, because I felt obligated to save him from suffocating in the middle of the night while I was out raiding the kitchen.

"I won't smother," he said.

"You will if I put all of my body weight on top of that pillow while it's over your face," I said.

This seemed to alarm him. "You wouldn't do that...?" he said.

"Well, I wouldn't if you were sleeping on it properly, I guess...," I said ominously.

I should know better than to argue with someone who has so much German stubbornness. It just made him all the more determined to keep doing exactly what he had been doing: mis-using his pillow. My only recourse is to shame him into proper pillow usage, so I've decided to start taking photos of him at night and posting them on what he calls the "Inter-Web."

Or, I could just sit on that pillow until he gets the message.

Food Service

I like to tell people I've never worked in food service.

I like to tell them that, but it's a lie.

It's not a lie designed to protect me, though. It's a lie to protect the reputation of the hardworking men and women who bring honor to the food service profession.

Yes, I put in my time in the restaurant business. It's just that my time totaled less than three days. As a result, I am just another clumsy, washed-up waiter who is now compelled to leave twenty-five percent tips for even the worst service, simply because I know how hard it is to sling hash.

I was fourteen years old when I decided I had outgrown lawn service, dog walking and pool care, even though it was our lawn, our dog and our pool. It was time to move up the corporate ladder.

My dad, in what I must assume was an effort to break my spirit completely or cause me to turn to drugs and gang violence, suggested I come to work for his construction company.

He shrugged when I told him I would rather not

because I didn't feel a particular "calling" to the construction business. I asked if I could get a job in a restaurant instead.

"Knock yourself out," he said, knowing full well that no restaurant that hoped to stay in business would ever hire me.

My first job application was as a waiter at the Denver Drumstick Restaurant, located fifteen minutes by bicycle from our house.

If I'd been hired, I would have been the only fourteen-year-old waiter at "The Drumstick," since all the servers at the time were at least seventy years old and wore hairnets and smart little paper hats. They were also women, so I could have broken through that glass ceiling as well.

The Drumstick, as the name implies, specialized in chicken. Fried chicken. What could be more glamourous than that? Even more appealing was the fact that this was the only restaurant in town which featured a model electric train hanging from the ceiling. This train, any kid's dream, navigated the perimeter of the dining room throughout the dinner hour. Kids begged their parents to go to the Drumstick to watch the train, even though the train didn't do anything but go around in circles. You couldn't ride it, after all, and you couldn't even fill it with sugar cubes because it was too high in the air. All you could do was follow its progress like Linda Blair's head in "The Exorcist:" 'round and 'round, until your crispy chicken arrived and you were forced to sit back down and "*eat, dammit!*"

Any place that was cool enough to have a model train was obviously a place I would like to work.

Unfortunately, the hostess who accepted my application didn't feel the same way, gently explaining that they wouldn't be hiring any fourteen-year-olds this season.

Next I went to the White Spot, where I gave my application to a fat guy with extremely bad breath who took one look at it and said, "D'ya ever wash dishes?"

"Sure," I lied, since I had once almost filled the dishwasher before my dad ordered me to stop because it was "women's work."

"Great. You start now. Come with me."

Talk about luck!

He motioned for me to follow him through a swinging door at the back of the dining room, but he pushed it so hard it flew back in my face and practically knocked me to the ground. He looked over his shoulder and sniggered but moved quickly as I trotted behind him.

In the far recesses of the kitchen I saw that I had my work cut out for me. There were stacks of dirty dishes and silverware completely covering a stainless steel countertop next to the dishwasher, and in plastic tubs all over the floor as well.

"Fired the last kid," he explained. "Lazy son-of-a-bitch couldn't keep up." He then leaned down and exhaled a stream of mustard gas into my face. "A word to the wise, kid. A word to the wise."

He grabbed a filthy apron from atop a stack of dirty dishes. "Here. Put this on."

I did as I was told as I watched him stumble through the piles of dishes on the floor until he stood to the left side of what looked like a miniature stainless steel garage perched in the middle of the counter. A long hose with a nozzle hung from the ceiling. He grabbed a plate and aimed the nozzle at it. When he squeezed, it shot a stream of pressurized water so strong that it knocked the plate out of his hand. It also sprayed the wall, the floor and, of course, me. When he fired the last kid he should have fired himself too.

"Shit!" he said, but at the same time he threw open the door of the mini-garage and pulled out a rolling rack. He threw the plate in it, shoved the rack back where it had just been, pulled the door down and flipped a switch. The resulting noise led me to believe the machine was crushing the plate, but in a minute or two he stepped to the other side, threw open the little door and pulled the rack out as steam billowed forth from the single, and now spotless, plate.

"There. Think you can do that?"

I wasn't so sure, but I nodded my head.

"Good. Get busy." And with that he was gone.

Ten hours later I was completely drenched in water and garbage. I hadn't had a break the entire time, and as fast as I worked, the piles of dishes never seemed to get any smaller. I could barely stand up.

Bad-breath guy reappeared -- the first time I'd seen him since I'd started -- and said, "Is that all you've done? You still have the trashcans to empty, y'know. There are six of 'em out on the floor, and they're all overflowing. Get your ass out there and take 'em to the dumpster out back.

I nodded dumbly and staggered toward the dining room, which was now empty, except for a couple of waitresses sitting in a booth toward the front, smoking cigarettes. I grabbed the nearest trashcan, and discovered it was so heavy I couldn't lift it. I dragged it behind me to the kitchen and then out the back door to the dumpster.

There was no way I could lift it to empty it. So I left it there, retrieved my bicycle from the side of the building where I'd left it ten hours earlier, and rode home. I never got a dime for my ten hours of work.

I now knew I hated the restaurant business, and vowed then and there that I would never work in another restaurant as long as I lived.

I kept my vow for almost five years. By then I was in my second year of college and desperate for money. My dad had cut me off because I dared to transfer from the college he had chosen and enrolled at the University of Colorado in Boulder instead.

"You're not going to that crazy place," he said.

"Yes, Dad. I am. I've applied, I've been accepted, and I'm going."

"Well, you'll do it on your own then. I won't be paying for it."

"Fine," I said. "I don't need your money."

But I did, of course. My grandmother helped some -- until my dad ordered her to stop -- so I had no choice but to get a job.

About the same time, one of my buddies told me about a new restaurant that was opening and said, "They're hiring waiters -- and you know waiters can pull down five or six hundred bucks a night." I knew his estimate was off by probably five or six hundred dollars, but I decided to apply anyway.

The Royal Knight was newly built and designed to look like a European castle, with turrets and a moat with a little bridge across it. Waiters and waitresses were referred to as knaves and wenches. The knaves had to wear a leather tunic that weighed about twelve pounds. Under the sleeveless tunic was a bright red satin shirt with big puffy sleeves, the very kind immortalized on an episode of *Seinfeld* some twenty years later.

I told the woman who was doing the hiring that I had restaurant experience, but that it had been several years ago, when I was just a "youngster." She gave me a look that seemed to say, "I think you're an idiot, but I'm going to hire you anyway because we need to get this joint open."

Our training the next day consisted mostly of food tastings so we could tell the customers how much we liked it. The only problem was, we didn't like it, because it tasted like crap.

We were told the following day was to be a "soft" opening -- without any advance publicity or advertising, just unlocking the doors to see if anybody wandered in. Several people did, but most of them were looking for the bank that had previously occupied this particular corner. When one of my co-workers offered to take an old lady's deposit, the manager put a sign on the door that said, "Not a bank." As we waited for more customers to stream in I thought of all the other signs he could put up: "Not a castle," "Not a car dealership," "Not a dentist's office," and so on. The possibilities were endless.

We were required to carry dishes on trays and it became quite a contest to see which of us could cram the most plates on the big metal tray before hoisting it up on our shoulder. That was the easy part. Keeping the plates on the tray was the tricky part.

The manager proudly told us that The Royal Knight had a varied menu, which included chicken, shrimp, spaghetti, pork chops, and hamburgers. It was varied, all right -- as long as you wanted your food deep fried.

The next day the advertising kicked in and we were slammed. It was my first full day as a waiter, and also my last. In the middle of service, I had a tray on my shoulder which was fully loaded with six plates -- two each of chicken, shrimp and spaghetti.

Half way to the table, I felt the plates begin to slide, and in a reflexive action to keep from dropping the tray, I threw it halfway across the restaurant. I am the first to admit that this was somewhat of an over-reaction, and honestly, I didn't mean to do it. Frankly, I didn't know I had the strength.

Pandemonium ensued. One woman, covered with spaghetti, screamed as others jumped to their feet, brushing chicken and shrimp from their clothing, leaving only greasy spots behind.

I stood in the middle of the restaurant, numb, wondering who had thrown that tray with such force. He must have been very strong, that's for sure.

While the hostess tried to restore order and began promising everybody that the restaurant would pay their dry cleaning costs, the manager took me by the arm -- rather forcibly, as I recall -- and dragged me back into the kitchen. He then "helped" me out of my tunic and pushed me out the back door into the alley.

I never got a dime for that job, either...but I did get to keep the puffy-sleeved red satin shirt, although I must say I have never had occasion to wear it.

From that day to this, every person who has ever served me in a restaurant has gotten a big, fat tip as my way of saying, "Thank you for not throwing the food at me."

Acknowledgements

If you go through this book and take out all the chapters with references to Brad Snyder, you will discover that you have a very thin book in your hand! So thanks, Brad, for being such a part of my life that I can try to make money by telling outrageous stories about you.

Thanks, too, to my children, Elisabeth and Jonathan, and their spouses, who, if they have read this far, are likely sitting in a state of shock, wondering if it's too late to call Social Services to make a report of bad parenting. My life has never been the same since they came along, and my sense of humor -- such that it is -- is largely attributed to the laughs they've given me over the years.

I don't know how I was ever able to write before I joined my two writing groups. Each one of these folks can write circles around me, and yet they humor me week after week and make me actually want to sit down at the computer. So, thank you: Richard Chapman, Sally Clark, and Stella Lillicrop in Denver; and, Katrina Bias, Pamela Farr-Collaro, Toni Hafey Smith, George Kubiak, Arlene Pascal, and Sylvia Selfman in Palm Springs.

Ten people provided expert counsel, advice and constructive criticism in their role of "advance readers" for this book. Trust me: you wouldn't have wanted to read it before they finished with it!

Thank you to Kim Cheeley (Coeur d'alene, ID), Suzy Ginsburg (Houston, TX), Christine Hook (Huntsville, TX), Thomas Keating (Lakewood, CO), Susan Liehe (Denver, CO), Stella Lillicrop (Greenwood Village, CO), Grace McCain (Nashville, TN), Tom Pagliasotti (Sandpoint, ID), Geoff Simpson (Lakewood, CO), and Florence Tallent (Rancho Mirage, CA). It would be polite to say that if any errors remain, they are mine and that you, dear reader, should blame me. But that's stupid. If any errors remain after these ten people made their corrections, you should hold them solely responsible!

Although I have officially denied it (so they can't sue me) I would be remiss not to thank several people who may have been, um, mentioned -- or alluded to -- in this book. They include my dear friends Marilyn and Larry Atler, John Bush and Greg Zarelli, Maria Bush, Donna Kolosky, Michael Luster, Linda Madigan, Susie Mammel, Elizabeth Percival and Stephanie Raymond.

Did you laugh?
Maybe your friends need a laugh, too!

Why not order another copy (or ten) of **The Pillow Goes Under Your Head** as gifts? It's easy: go to amazon.com — available in printed form or for e-readers.

You might also enjoy…
…these other works by Rex John

Makeovers - Carson Kirkpatrick doesn't like the way the world is going. People are lazy and stupid. Worse, they are unkempt and bad-mannered. Something must be done and he -- born to power and privilege -- is just the person to do it. *"I recommend this thriller to anyone who enjoys their crime fiction with a touch of humor."* - G.S., Lakewood, CO

Available at **Amazon.com, smashwords.com, iTunes,** or your local bookstore.

The Flying Shoe - Trevor is new to Portland and needs to make friends. When he meets Sean, Amy, and Nate -- scruffy street kids who hang out at a local coffee shop -- he makes an effort to befriend them. Sean is full of attitude, but he needs Trevor's help to solve a problem that involves five dollars, a death, and a "borrowed" car." *-"A great, short read!"* - C.H., Huntsville, TX - *"Engaging! That's all I will say because I don't want to give away the end."* - H.H., Denver, CO

Available as an e-book from **Amazon.com** or **smashwords.com**

REX JOHN

www.ingramcontent.com/pod-product-compliance
Lightning Source LLC
Chambersburg PA
CBHW071523040426
42452CB00008B/864